Empowering Young Readers

Empowering Young Readers

Dialogic Reading with Integrated Vocabulary Enrichment

Dina Moore and Cheryl C. Durwin

ROWMAN & LITTLEFIELD
Lanham • Boulder • New York • London

Published by Rowman & Littlefield
An imprint of The Rowman & Littlefield Publishing Group, Inc.
4501 Forbes Boulevard, Suite 200, Lanham, Maryland 20706
www.rowman.com

86-90 Paul Street, London EC2A 4NE, United Kingdom

Copyright © 2022 by Dina Moore and Cheryl C. Durwin

All rights reserved. No part of this book may be reproduced in any form or by any electronic or mechanical means, including information storage and retrieval systems, without written permission from the publisher, except by a reviewer who may quote passages in a review.

British Library Cataloguing in Publication Information Available

Library of Congress Cataloging-in-Publication Data

Names: Moore, Dina, 1972- author. | Durwin, Cheryl Cisero, author.
Title: Empowering young readers : dialogic reading with integrated vocabulary enrichment / Dina Moore, Cheryl C. Durwin.
Description: Lanham, Maryland : Rowman & Littlefield Publishing Group, [2022] | Includes bibliographical references and index. | Summary: "Anyone who reads with young children will benefit from this book designed to provide a fun, evidence-based approach to shared reading. Empowering Young Readers offers a straightforward approach for creating meaningful dialogues while reading as well as practical recommendations for getting the most out of your cherished reading experiences"—Provided by publisher.
Identifiers: LCCN 2022024732 (print) | LCCN 2022024733 (ebook) | ISBN 9781475864380 (Cloth) | ISBN 9781475864397 (Paperback) | ISBN 9781475864403 (epub)
Subjects: LCSH: Oral reading. | Storytelling. | Children—Books and reading. | Reading. | Vocabulary—Study and teaching.
Classification: LCC LB1573.5 .M665 2022 (print) | LCC LB1573.5 (ebook) | DDC 372.45/2—dc23/eng/20220708
LC record available at https://lccn.loc.gov/2022024732
LC ebook record available at https://lccn.loc.gov/2022024733

We would like to dedicate this book to our children, Nate and Amelia Brancazio and Mark and Andrea Durwin. Thank you for our shared reading time and the books we came to love together.

Contents

Foreword		ix
Preface		xi
Acknowledgments		xvii
Introduction: The Importance of Shared Reading		xix
1	How Do Children Become Good Readers?	1
2	What Is the DRIVE Approach?	13
3	Overview of EMPOWERED Strategies	25
4	Encouraging Vocabulary	41
5	Choosing a Book	53
6	Tips to Consider while Reading	65
7	Closing Thoughts	79
Bibliography		89
Index		101
About the Authors		103

Foreword

Elevating the conversation beyond simply reading to the children in your life, *Empowering Young Readers: Dialogic Reading with Integrated Vocabulary Enrichment* illuminates the importance of the *quality* of the book-reading experience. Caregiver-child shared book reading supports both language and reading development, providing a critical foundation for reading achievement. By outlining the skills required for children to become good readers and providing specific approaches to employ during shared book reading, this volume will be transformative for caregivers and professionals alike. Critically, the techniques provided in this much-needed volume also outline a method of intervention for children at risk for reading failure.

    Developed from the authors' successful reading program in primary schools, this book presents a research-based technique called Dialogic Reading with Integrated Vocabulary Enrichment. Dialogic reading refers to shared book-reading that involves active back-and-forth engagement with the child, emphasizing reciprocal conversation, vocabulary learning, and building an understanding of the story. This book begins by introducing the reader to the underlying skills needed to read fluently and comprehend what was read and goes beyond to provide explicit strategies using the acronym EMPOWERED to show the specific practices to use during dialogic reading. These strategies literally empower both the caregiver and the child during shared book reading by encouraging positive responses and open-ended questions that deepen the child's engagement and understanding, helping them connect more deeply with the story.

The powerful set of strategies outlined in this book can be used during shared book reading with children by caregivers or professionals across a range of ages and can ameliorate potential delays. A must have for parents, grandparents, educators, reading specialists, and librarians, *Empowering Young Readers: Dialogic Reading with Integrated Vocabulary Enrichment* places children as active participants in their own understanding of narratives, vocabulary development, and constructing meaning.

Julia Irwin
Professor of Psychology, Southern Connecticut State University
Senior Scientist, Haskins Laboratories

Preface

Empowering Young Readers: Dialogic Reading with Integrated Vocabulary Enrichment presents a shared reading approach that involves creating a rich dialogue between an adult and child while reading, which will help parents, caregivers, teachers, and other adults promote oral vocabulary development and reading comprehension in their children as well as an intrinsic enjoyment of reading.

Formal reading instruction begins when children enter school; however, the road to becoming a good reader starts long before children board their first school bus. Hearing language, seeing, and interacting with print and books, and, importantly, being read to set the stage for early literacy development. This caregiver-child shared book reading fosters language and reading development and provides an important foundation for later reading achievement and ongoing motivation to read.

Reading to young children can take many forms. We read to infants and toddlers using simple board books that teach children letters, numbers, shapes, and objects. We read nursery rhymes and other rhyming books. We read picture story books that vary in their complexity, some with very simple sentences, actions, and plot, often used with younger children, and other books with a rich, elaborate story structure. All of these types of shared reading contribute to and foster reading development.

There are also many ways to engage in shared book reading with children, and adults vary in their approach. Some use more of a storytelling style where the adult assumes a narrator role and child takes on the role of listener. In this style, children are expected to listen attentively and not interrupt the storytelling. This may be typical when reading to a group of children at library story hour or when a tired parent reads a book before bedtime.

Other adults use more of a *storybuilding* style that promotes active child participation and interactive conversation. In this style, adults take on the role of co-narrator and create a back-and-forth dialogue involving questions and answers to help children build an understanding of the story. This storybuilding style typically resembles the types of interactions between teachers and students in schools when reading. It is this second type of storybuilding style, where the adult and child engage in a dialogue, that is the basis for the approach, called Dialogic Reading with Integrated Vocabulary Enrichment or DRIVE, discussed in this book.

We developed this approach based on our research collaboration with schools serving large populations of primary school children (K–3) from lower-socioeconomic backgrounds. These schools were faced with the daunting task of meeting the overwhelming needs of many children who were struggling to read. The goal of our research was to help schools improve the reading skills of their at-risk readers.

The first step was to figure out what the struggling readers needed. We wanted to design an intervention that was evidence-based and that targeted the underlying difficulties of individual children. Based on the data we collected, we found that the schools were successful at improving some of these students' critical reading skills, such as knowledge about print, phonological skills, and word recognition (topics to be discussed in more detail in chapter 1). However, many of their struggling readers in the early grades lacked adequate oral vocabulary and prior knowledge about common events in stories which are necessary to support comprehension.

Based on these findings, we chose a research-based technique called dialogic reading to use in the schools. The original technique was designed for preschool children and trained parents and preschool teachers to read with children using the storybuilding style in order to promote comprehension. To work with older children, we modified some of the strategies used and added an emphasis on vocabulary enrichment.

In order to work with as many children in the schools as possible, we trained our own young undergraduate students many of whom had never read to a child before. The result of this work has led to an evidence-based and effective approach that we believe any adult can learn to use to help young readers from many different backgrounds develop into skilled readers.

In this book we provide step-by-step descriptions of the strategies used to implement our approach both when reading to an individual child as well as a small group of children. We share sample dialogues that you can use as a guide to engage in a conversation about a book that will support vocabulary development and reading comprehension. We also offer many examples of vocabulary words and book titles to get you started. All of our sample dialogue and vocabulary suggestions are based on hands-on experiences gathered from our undergraduates who have successfully used the approach in schools over many years of our research.

We wrote this book for parents and caregivers, early childhood teachers, paraprofessionals working in primary grades, librarians, and really anyone who wants to take an active role in supporting literacy development of young children. *Empowering Young Readers: Dialogic Reading with Integrated Vocabulary Enrichment* will help you to enrich children's reading experiences, support word learning, and create a lasting impact on their love of reading.

ORGANIZATION

Before introducing the approach outlined in this book, we first discuss the crucial foundations that children need to become skilled readers. Starting with the Introduction, "The Importance of Shared Reading," we familiarize readers with why shared book reading is such a critical component of an enriching literacy environment. In chapter 1 "How Do Children Become Good Readers?" we provide an overview of the many skills that children need to acquire in order to become good readers—that is, to be able to read fluently and understand what is read. While all of these skills are equally important and work together, our dialogic reading approach outlined in this book focuses on two key skills: vocabulary and comprehension.

The introduction to our approach begins in chapter 2, "What Is the DRIVE Approach?" Here we provide an overview of DRIVE and introduce the strategies used to engage in dialogic reading. These strategies will be outlined in more detail in subsequent chapters. As DRIVE is an evidence-based approach, we end the chapter with a summary of some of the research that led to its development as well as evidence for its effectiveness in supporting vocabulary development and reading comprehension.

Chapter 3, "Overview of EMPOWERED Strategies," gives the reader a more thorough how-to explanation of each of the strategies that are a part of the DRIVE approach. We refer to these strategies using the acronym EMPOWERED. In addition to explaining each strategy, several examples are provided using excerpts from two children's books. We offer detailed, practical advice so that readers can feel confident in using our approach on their own.

As the DRIVE approach was specifically designed to support vocabulary knowledge, chapter 4, "Encouraging Vocabulary," explores why vocabulary is so important for reading and how children acquire new words. In this chapter, readers will learn what vocabulary words are best to focus on when using the DRIVE approach and how to encourage vocabulary using some of the EMPOWERED strategies outlined in chapter 3. This chapter also provides sample book suggestions as well as accompanying vocabulary words.

Throughout the book we provide you with many examples of wonderful children's books, both classic and new, to get you started. However, we don't expect that you will rely only on these titles. Book choice is driven by many factors such as the age of the child, attention span, and interests. But how do you know which books are right for DRIVE? While there are no specific criteria that determine which book is right, there are certain elements that make a book a better choice, such as an engaging story and rich vocabulary. In chapter 5, "Choosing a Book," we offer a set of guidelines to help you choose the right book for an individual child or a small group of children you are reading with.

Once you have learned about the DRIVE approach, its EMPOWERED strategies, and how to choose an appropriate book, chapter 6, "Tips to Consider while Reading," provides additional general tips for use during DRIVE. We offer suggestions on very practical topics such as how long to read in a given session and how long to wait for a child to respond, as well as how to use pictures as an aid for comprehension.

We also offer further advice on the types of questions that you can use to encourage children to engage in a conversation and how to provide scaffolding when children are either hesitant to answer questions or provide incomplete responses. This chapter ends with a special section for educators, librarians, or anyone who may be reading to a group of children to adjust the approach for a small group.

Finally, chapter 7, "Closing Thoughts," concludes with an opportunity for the reader to further examine DRIVE in action (and practice on their own) with two additional sample scripts. Additionally, we provide readers with resources including books, articles, and links to video clips demonstrating shared reading.

The goal of shared reading is to foster an interactive and engaging dialogue that will help children build an understanding of a story. *Empowering Young Readers: Dialogic Reading with Integrated Vocabulary Enrichment* gives adults a repertoire of evidence-based strategies that can help promote the development of vocabulary and reading comprehension in young children.

Acknowledgments

We are grateful to the many children in the schools where we have worked for allowing us to read with you. We have learned so much from our time with you. We would like to especially thank the teachers, staff, and principals for their dedication to literacy and for their support in implementing our reading approach. We are truly indebted to the many undergraduate students who have served as our research assistants over the years whose direct work with the children in schools and feedback helped shape the development of our reading approach. A special thank you to Stephanie Kaesmann, our current graduate student, who provided invaluable feedback on drafts of this book.

Introduction
The Importance of Shared Reading

Becoming a good reader begins long before children enter school. It starts with an enriching home literacy environment. This includes access to books and caregivers who spend time reading with children and engaging in other literacy activities, such as singing, rhyming, playing word games, storytelling, and writing.[1]

The amount of time that parents and caregivers spend reading books with their young children impacts children's oral language development and their early literacy skills, such as print awareness, phonological awareness, knowledge of letters and their sounds, and word recognition.[2,3] Frequent shared book reading with young children also promotes vocabulary development, fosters an intrinsic motivation to read, and contributes to reading achievement and general academic achievement in the elementary school years.[4,5]

It is not just the amount of shared book reading that is important, but also the quality of the book-reading experience. Generally speaking, a shared book reading style that encourages active participation from the child and emphasizes conversation about the story is most beneficial for promoting children's oral language and comprehension.[6] The back-and-forth dialogue of a conversation encourages children to actively construct an understanding of the story.[7] This style of communication typically resembles the types of interactions in schools between teachers and students during reading sessions.[8]

In many American families, parents and caregivers typically begin shared book reading when children are about six months of age.[9]

However, there is a great deal of variability from family to family depending on their circumstances. In some families experiencing socioeconomic adversity, there is less access to books and learning materials, and caregivers tend to spend less time in shared reading activities.[10]

Even if children are not initially exposed to shared reading in the home, they can benefit from interventions that train parents and teachers to use this approach.

- Training parents to use shared book reading with children ranging in age from about eight months through five years has resulted in improvements in children's vocabulary.[11]
- Training teachers to implement shared reading interventions with children ages three through eight who are at risk for reading difficulties has yielded improvements in children's phonological awareness (the understanding that spoken words are made up of individual sounds), print concepts, vocabulary, and comprehension.[12]

Many research studies have used various shared reading approaches, with some training only parents, some only teachers, and others using a combined intervention involving both parents and teachers. Across all these approaches, some conclusions regarding the effectiveness of shared book reading interventions can be made.

- These interventions can enhance children's development of oral language skills, particularly vocabulary and comprehension.[13]
- Benefits are observed for preschool-age children as well as kindergarteners and older children at risk for reading difficulties and for children from various ethnic and socioeconomic backgrounds.[14,15]
- Particular benefits have been found for improving the literacy outcomes of children from lower-socioeconomic backgrounds.[16]
- Shared book reading approaches that are more interactive have been found to be more effective in improving literacy outcomes than less interactive read-aloud methods.[17]

One specific type of interactive shared book reading approach that has been extensively studied is called dialogic reading. In dialogic reading, the adult and child engage in a dialogue about the story. Adults ask questions that encourage the child to participate in a conversation about the story, they model more complex language for the child, and they use various techniques to encourage the child to develop more complex vocabulary and language expression. In general, research studies have found dialogic reading to be effective for improving children's vocabulary, oral language, reading comprehension, and early literacy skills, especially for those at risk for reading difficulties.[18,19]

In this book, parents, caregivers, early childhood teachers, librarians, and any adults who work with young children will learn about a specific dialogic reading approach called Dialogic Reading with Integrated Vocabulary Enrichment, or DRIVE. This approach is based on the original dialogic reading intervention that has been extensively researched and found to be an effective shared book reading technique for children from preschool through the primary grades.

The DRIVE approach can be used with preschool children, beginning readers, and children in the primary grades who are struggling with comprehension. This approach can be used one-on-one as well as in small groups, which makes it useful for early childhood educators, librarians, and paraprofessionals in addition to parents and caregivers.

Even though the DRIVE approach can be used as an intervention in schools, it is not a reading or literacy curriculum (often called English Language Arts curriculum in elementary schools). The type of reading curriculum that a child receives in the classroom will depend on the school and district that a child attends. School districts often purchase commercial curriculum packages that specify the content that will be covered and the method of instruction for both reading and math.

An effective curriculum will address key components of skilled reading: phonemic awareness, phonics, fluency, vocabulary, and comprehension. School districts should publicize the curriculum in use and concerned parents and caregivers can check the district website where their child attends school to identify the literacy curriculum that is used to teach reading. As noted above, research in the science of reading has specified what makes a reading curriculum effective.

However, even when the curriculum being used addresses the key components necessary for skilled reading, sometimes children will need extra support outside of the classroom curriculum to develop one or more of these components. DRIVE is one approach that paraprofessionals and school volunteers can use to supplement reading instruction for struggling readers. It can also be used by parents, caregivers, librarians, and anyone who reads to children to promote reading development outside of school.

Before learning about the DRIVE approach, it is important to understand how children become good readers. In chapter 1, you will learn about the critical skills that help children become good readers. To be prepared for reading instruction, young children need to develop skills at identifying letters and their sounds, phonological awareness, and concepts about print.

As they are exposed to reading, both formally, through instruction in school, and informally through reading with parents and caregivers at home, children begin to develop skills, such as word recognition, decoding (sounding out words), vocabulary, and comprehension. All of these important foundational skills will be discussed in chapter 1. This book focuses on how to encourage development of vocabulary and comprehension.

In subsequent chapters, you will learn how the DRIVE approach can improve children's oral language and comprehension, and how to use the specific strategies that comprise this approach, with a particular emphasis on how to employ DRIVE strategies. You will also learn how to choose books that are appropriate for dialogic reading and general tips to consider for successful one-on-one and small-group reading sessions. The book concludes with some final thoughts on implementing DRIVE and provides readers with resources such as additional literacy-related books, reader-friendly articles, websites, and organizations for obtaining books for children.

NOTES

1. Suzanne E. Mol and Adriana G. Bus. "To Read or Not to Read: A Meta-Analysis of Print Exposure From Infancy to Early Adulthood." *Psychological Bulletin* 137, no. 2 (2011): 267–96. doi: 10.1037/a0021890.

2. Erica Barnes and Jaime Puccioni. "Shared Book Reading and Preschool Children's Academic Achievement: Evidence from the Early Childhood Longitudinal Study—Birth Cohort." *Infant and Child Development* 26, no. 6 (2017): 1–20. doi: 10.1002/icd.2035.

3. Suzanne E. Mol, Adriana G. Bus, and Maria T. de Jong. "Interactive Book Reading in Early Education: A Tool to Stimulate Print Knowledge as

Well as Oral Language." *Review of Educational Research* 79, no. 2 (2009): 979–1007. doi: 10.3102/0034654309332561.

4. Allen W. Gottfried, Jonah Schlackman, Adele Eskeles Gottfried, and Alma S. Boutin-Martinez. "Parental Provision of Early Literacy Environment as Related to Reading and Educational Outcomes Across the Academic Lifespan." *Parenting* 15, no. 1 (2015): 24–38. doi: 10.1080/15295192.2015.992736.

5. Joseph Price and Ariel Kalil. "The Effect of Mother–Child Reading Time on Children's Reading Skills: Evidence From Natural Within-Family Variation." *Child Development* 90, no. 6 (2019): e688–702. doi: 10.1111/cdev.13137.

6. Keely D. Cline and Carolyn Pope Edwards. "Parent–Child Book-Reading Styles, Emotional Quality, and Changes in Early Head Start Children's Cognitive Scores." *Early Education and Development* 28, no. 1 (2017): 41–58. doi: 10.1080/10409289.2016.1177392.

7. Ibid.

8. Gigliana Melzi and Margaret Caspe. "Variations in Maternal Narrative Styles during Book Reading Interactions." *Narrative Inquiry* 15, no. 1 (2005): 101–25. doi: 10.1075/ni.15.1.06mel.

9. Anne van Kleek. "Cultural Issues in Promoting Interactive Book Sharing." In *Sharing Books and Stories to Promote Language and Literacy*, ed. Anne van Kleek (San Diego, CA: Plural, 2006), 179–230.

10. Nicholas Dowdall, G. J. Melendez-Torres, Lynne Murray, Frances Gardner, Leila Hartford, and Peter J. Cooper. "Shared Picture Book Reading Interventions for Child Language Development: A Systematic Review and Meta-Analysis." *Child Development* 91, no. 2 (2020): e383–99. doi: 10.1111/cdev.13225.

11. Ibid.

12. Elizabeth Swanson, Sharon Vaughn, Jeanne Wanzek, Yaacov Petscher, Jennifer Heckert, Christie Cavanaugh, Guliz Kraft, and Kathryn Tackett. "A Synthesis of Read-Aloud Interventions on Early Reading Outcomes among Preschool through Third Graders at Risk for Reading Difficulties." *Journal of Learning Disabilities* 44, no. 3 (2011): 258–75. doi:10.1177/0022219410378444.

13. Dowdall et al., "Shared Picture Book Reading Interventions for Child Language Development: A Systematic Review and Meta-Analysis."

14. Christopher Lonigan, Timothy Shanahan, and Anne Cunningham. *Impact of Shared-Reading Interventions on Young Children's Early Literacy Skills*. Developing Early Literacy: Report of the National Early Literacy Panel, In Eunice Kennedy Shriver National Institute of Child Health and Human Development, NIH, DHHS (Washington, DC: U.S. Government Printing Office, 2008), 153–171.

15. Swanson et al., "A Synthesis of Read-Aloud Interventions on Early Reading Outcomes among Preschool through Third Graders at Risk for Reading Difficulties."
16. Lonigan et al., *Impact of Shared-Reading Interventions on Young Children's Early Literacy Skills.*
17. Swanson et al., "A Synthesis of Read-Aloud Interventions on Early Reading Outcomes among Preschool through Third Graders at Risk for Reading Difficulties."
18. Lonigan et al., *Impact of Shared-Reading Interventions on Young Children's Early Literacy Skills.*
19. Swanson et al., "A Synthesis of Read-Aloud Interventions on Early Reading Outcomes among Preschool through Third Graders at Risk for Reading Difficulties."

Chapter 1

How Do Children Become Good Readers?

This book presents an approach for engaging in shared reading with young children that can promote the development of vocabulary and reading comprehension. However, vocabulary and comprehension are only some of the components of becoming a good reader. Before discussing the particular approach outlined in this book, it is important to begin with what is known about the key skills for becoming a good reader. Evidence from reading research can tell educators, librarians, parents, and caregivers a lot about what makes a successful reader.

First, what is a *good* reader? In thinking about reading and what it means to be a good reader, the emphasis is usually on reading comprehension. Simply put, a good reader is able to easily *understand* what they have read. While comprehension is the ultimate goal or outcome, obviously there are other skills or building blocks that underlie successful reading development.

One widely accepted view of reading comes from researchers Gough and Tunmer.[1] According to their *simple view of reading*, reading comprehension is the result of two basic abilities, decoding skills and language comprehension; where decoding is the ability to sound out the printed words and language comprehension is the ability to understand and make sense of *spoken* language. In the simple view, while decoding and language comprehension are seen as separate skills, and individuals may differ in these abilities, these two components also interact with each other.

For a skilled adult reader, the process of reading is seemingly effortless. Experienced readers can quickly recognize words, access their meanings, and comprehend what they have read. But for many readers, young and old, this process is not so easy. And even the simple view of reading is not as simple as it seems. In fact, there are many processes that underlie a reader's ability to both decode and comprehend. Research in reading development and the science of reading has shown that there are a set of crucial skills which are necessary for reading success.[2,3]

Many of these skills begin to develop prior to formal reading instruction in school and they highlight the importance of a developing reader's oral language (both speaking and listening). And some of these critical components require explicit instruction, usually in the classroom, by a trained teacher (e.g., phonics which will be discussed below). But because reading is complex, and relies on building blocks such as oral language skills, background knowledge, and vocabulary, there are many things that can be done outside of the classroom, or to supplement classroom instruction, that can aid reading development.

The following sections will provide a brief overview of early pre-reading skills (alphabet knowledge, book handling skills, concepts about print), phonological awareness, phonemic awareness and the alphabetic principle, automatic word recognition, phonics instruction, fluency, vocabulary, and comprehension.

EARLY PRE-READING SKILLS

An early precursor to emerging literacy is alphabet knowledge. Alphabet knowledge is the ability to visually recognize and name letters. This is an important skill in the acquisition of literacy, as children need to be able to recognize letters before they can work on sounding them out in printed words. Research has shown that alphabet knowledge in preschool and kindergarten is predictive of later reading skills.[4,5] Obviously, children will need more than just letter identification to become skilled readers, but alphabet knowledge is a good start.

Basic experiences with books and text also can help emergent readers become prepared for reading instruction. Book handling skills involve knowing what a book is and how to use it. This can include understanding what is the front of the book and what is the back and differences between pictures and text. A young child who understands and has knowledge of how to interact with a book will likely have had exposure to books and engaged in shared reading with an adult. This early exposure can begin to set the stage for emerging literacy.

Related to book handling and knowledge about books is concepts about print which is an understanding that it is the words on the page that are important. Specifically, a pre-reader needs to understand that the reader is not just making up or telling the story from memory, but rather they are using the text on the page. From concepts about print, a child will eventually move to a speech-to-print match as they learn to read themselves.

Children who have alphabet knowledge, book handling skills, and concepts about print will still need to develop other skills (discussed below) to become successful readers. But these pre-reading skills are crucial in reading development and highlight the importance of the environment on reading development. Being actively read to by a parent or caregiver and having exposure to a literate environment in which young children have access to books and print will support the development of these pre-reading skills.

PHONOLOGICAL AWARENESS

While alphabet knowledge is a foundation for reading development, just visually recognizing the alphabet is not enough. To read, children will also need to know that the letters, known as graphemes, represent sounds, known as phonemes. Critically, children need to learn grapheme-phoneme correspondences (or the alphabetic principle). However, it turns out that before learning the alphabetic principle, children first need the ability to work with sounds in *spoken* language. Specifically, children need to develop phonological awareness.

The importance of phonological awareness in reading development cannot be stressed enough. And while the dialogic reading approach that will be outlined in this book does not specifically address phonological awareness, adults working with young children should have an understanding of this crucial skill.

Phonological awareness is broadly defined as the understanding that spoken words are made up of individual sounds, called phonemes. Phonemes are described as the building blocks of language, the smallest units of sound that can change the meaning of a word. For example, the spoken English word "cat" is made up of three phonemes /k/ /a/ /t/. Changing one of these phonemes can change the meaning of the word. For example, changing the /k/ in cat to a /b/ creates the word "bat." While different languages may have fewer, more, or different phonemes from each other, phonemes form the basis of all spoken languages.

Awareness of the *spoken* sounds of a language develops throughout childhood, often beginning before formal schooling (and reading instruction) and continuing to develop well into early elementary school. For most children, phonological awareness follows a relatively similar timeline with phonological sensitivity emerging before the more complex phonemic awareness.

Phonological sensitivity refers to the ability to notice more large-grain similarities in the sounds of words. It is as simple as understanding that the word *dinosaur* is longer than the word *cat*. However, it also includes an understanding of syllables (the word *dog* has fewer syllables than the word *dandelion*) and rhyme (the words *cat* and *hat* rhyme). Phonological sensitivity can be seen in children as young as preschool and is a precursor to the more developmentally complex and fine-grained phonemic awareness.

With phonemic awareness, children are able to recognize that words are made up of individual consonant and vowel sounds. Even though speakers of a language can easily produce and understand phonemes while speaking and listening in conversations, the ability to identify individual phonemes in spoken words is not always easy. Phonemic awareness will continue to develop throughout early childhood, often together with early literacy. And phonemic awareness almost always requires explicit instruction as a child is learning to read.[6,7]

It is important to note that phonological awareness does not necessarily mean that a child is reading. However, it does enable a child to learn the alphabetic principle, the understanding that we use letters and letter patterns (graphemes) to represent the spoken sounds of language (phonemes). And learning the relationship between graphemes and phonemes is the key to acquiring skill at decoding which allows children to sound out written words.

There is much research to support the importance of phonological awareness in learning to read. For example, children who have some phonological awareness early (at ages four and five) before learning to read show better reading skills in later grades.[8] And training in phonological awareness before learning to read also results in better reading skills later on.[9] Finally, well beyond early elementary school, the awareness of phonemes distinguishes more skilled readers from less skilled ones.[10]

AUTOMATIC WORD RECOGNITION

As noted above, the development of reading requires that children learn the alphabetic principle in order to decode (sound out) the printed word. Knowing the relationship between graphemes and phonemes is one powerful strategy that readers can use to read unfamiliar words. For a fluent, skilled reader, the process of decoding has become automatic and word recognition is not solely dependent on sounding out words phoneme by phoneme. As reading skill develops, readers can bring together their knowledge of phonemes in spoken words, spelling patterns (also known as orthography), and word meanings to quickly and accurately recognize and comprehend words.

Through the process referred to as orthographic mapping, children can commit words to memory so that the sight of the word automatically elicits its pronunciation as well as its meaning.[11] Having access to many of these "sight words" allows a child to develop more automatic word recognition skills which is essential in the development of fluency. Strong decoding skills together with the development of orthographic mapping will allow developing readers to instantly recognize many unfamiliar as well as familiar words.

PHONICS INSTRUCTION

Given the importance of phonological awareness in learning to read, and the challenges that children may face in "cracking the code" (i.e., learning the alphabetic principle), children need to be taught to read using systematic and explicit phonics-based methods. Specifically, children need to be taught grapheme-phoneme (letter-sound) correspondences and patterns of spelling. There is extensive evidence to support that phonics-based instruction helps children to read more effectively than other methods.[12,13]

And while all children benefit from phonics instruction beginning as early as kindergarten, for children who are having difficulty learning to read or who may be at risk for reading difficulties, systematic phonics instruction is particularly important. Finally, systematic phonics instruction does not just improve a child's ability to decode words, it has also been shown to improve early readers' comprehension ability.[14]

FLUENCY

As children are learning to read and becoming more skilled readers, another essential component of literacy is the development of fluency. Fluency is the ability to read quickly, with accuracy and while maintaining proper expression. A fluent reader can quickly identify words, but fluency refers to more than just single word reading; it refers to the sentence level and beyond, and incorporates the ability to read connected text in meaningful units. The development of fluency is important because it is an indicator of decoding ability, that is, how easily a child can sound out a word.

More importantly, fluent reading is also tied to measures of reading comprehension. Specifically, children who struggle with fluency are likely also to struggle with understanding what they have read.[15] Halting word-by-word reading is effortful and takes time. If a child is using all of their cognitive resources to simply decode words, then there is going to be less effort available to understand what is being read. Research has shown that, with the right kind of instruction, fluency can be taught. Specifically, techniques which include independent oral reading that encourage repetition and where the child is given guidance or feedback from a teacher can lead to improvements in fluency.[16,17]

VOCABULARY

The importance of vocabulary, or knowledge of word meanings, in reading achievement is discussed in more detail in chapter 4 as vocabulary enrichment is emphasized in the approach that will be outlined in this book. However, this section provides an overview of vocabulary knowledge and its relationship to reading development and skill.

Vocabulary knowledge can be broken down into receptive vocabulary (the words a child recognizes or understands) and expressive

How Do Children Become Good Readers?

vocabulary (the words that a child can produce to label objects around them). Research investigating the role of vocabulary (knowledge of word meanings) has shown a relationship with both decoding ability as well as reading comprehension.[18] And while both expressive and receptive vocabulary knowledge contribute to reading development, the ability to produce the correct labels—that is, expressive vocabulary—has been shown to be the strongest predictor.[19]

In addition to examining differences in expressive and receptive word knowledge, researchers have also investigated the distinction between vocabulary breadth, defined as the number of words that a child knows, and vocabulary depth, defined as how well the child knows particular words. This distinction illustrates that a child may have a word in their mental dictionary (breadth) without having a completely developed understanding of what the word actually means (depth). Both vocabulary breadth and depth independently contribute to the development of reading skills with the breadth of receptive vocabulary showing relationships with decoding ability and depth with reading comprehension.[20]

Much vocabulary knowledge is acquired through incidental learning, that is picking up on word meanings through exposure to hearing the words in spoken language. And there is substantial evidence that children who are exposed to more words in their oral language environment tend to know more words.[21,22] But vocabulary instruction in school can lead to further vocabulary development as well as improved reading comprehension. Importantly, both explicit methods of vocabulary instruction (directly teaching word meanings, for example) as well as more indirect methods (such as reading to children) lead to increases in vocabulary growth as well as reading comprehension.[23,24]

What is important to emphasize in vocabulary instruction? Again, this will be discussed in more detail in chapter 4, but what follows are a few key points to keep in mind. First and most obviously, the child needs to have a general conceptual understanding of vocabulary words. This does not mean that the child needs to provide a dictionary definition, but that their usage indicates that they generally understand what the word means. For example, if a child says that "*greedy* is when you take too many cookies," this indicates that they have a general idea of what the word means. The focus of instruction would be to help them to understand that the word greedy can apply not just to taking too much food, but that it is when you want or take too much of anything.

Additionally, the child needs to have an accurate and precise pronunciation of the word. This is important for decoding the word in print as it is difficult to sound out a word in print if the child cannot accurately pronounce the word. Finally, the child should be able to access the word across a range of different contexts. For example, the word *bright* can mean the amount of light given off, but also how intelligent or clever a person might be. Having access to multiple meanings of a word will make it easier for the child to comprehend what they read.

Vocabulary knowledge is important across all developmental reading levels. However, as children move from learning to read to reading to learn (i.e., to specifically gain knowledge on their own through reading) around Grade 3 and beyond, vocabulary knowledge becomes increasingly important in reading comprehension. Simply put, knowing more words will be beneficial and will impact a child's ability to comprehend complex text.

READING COMPREHENSION

The ultimate goal of reading is comprehension, an understanding of what is being read. As noted above, reading to learn new things, both in academic life and outside of school, becomes increasingly important with the development of reading skills. Not surprisingly, if a child is struggling with any of the other components or skills previously discussed, it may negatively affect comprehension.

For some children, difficulty with comprehension is a result of poor decoding skills coupled with less fluent reading. A child who is struggling with decoding will simply have fewer attentional resources to devote to understanding what is read. Other children, however, may have adequate decoding skills but still struggle with comprehending what is read. For these children the difficulty may lie in oral language skills such as listening comprehension and vocabulary.[25,26] Additionally, comprehension may be difficult for children if they lack background knowledge about the outside world.[27]

Vocabulary, background knowledge, and comprehension interact with one another, and difficulty with one component can result in challenges with another. A child who knows fewer words may have a difficult time understanding what is being read. And they likely may also have a hard time decoding the words in the first place, as it is challenging to read words if you haven't heard or seen them before.

The words a child knows, especially in terms of their expressive vocabulary, also gives some insight into the types of experiences or background knowledge that the child has. If a child knows and can produce the word *erupt*, for example, this suggests that they might have background knowledge about volcanoes. Having knowledge of word meanings and background knowledge together will aid them in their comprehension when reading or being read to.

Children vary dramatically in the number of words they know when they begin to learn to read. Typically achieving children learn approximately 3,000 new words per year; however, this value can range from 1,000 to 5,000 words.[28] As noted above, knowing fewer words can contribute to difficulties with both decoding and comprehension. Crucially, if these differences are not addressed, it can have a snowball effect on reading acquisition and skill. Continued difficulty with word recognition and understanding what is being read may lead a child to read less which further hinders reading development.

This complex relationship between reading experience and reading skill is described by Stanovich as the Matthew Effect (i.e., the rich get richer and the poor get poorer).[29] Children who are exposed to and know fewer words may read less because it is difficult, and in turn are then exposed to fewer words. Sobering data from Nagy and Anderson supports this with estimates that by middle grades less skilled readers read approximately 100,000 words per year in school while the most skilled readers read anywhere from 10,000,000 to 50,000,000.[30] Simply reading more means that the most skilled reader is being exposed to more words and background knowledge, which gives them more practice with word recognition and also contributes to their overall comprehension of what is being read.

SUMMARY

The development of skilled reading, where an individual is easily able to decode words and has access to the vocabulary and background knowledge necessary for reading comprehension, is not as simple as the simple view of reading might imply. As noted in this chapter, there are many skills that are necessary for successful reading development. It should also be clear that while these skills may develop separately, they are not isolated from one another.

For example, a child who has heard a word spoken often will have an easier time sounding out and recognizing that word later on. Similarly, phonics instruction will be easier for the child who has strong phonological skills prior to learning to read. And vocabulary knowledge (both knowing what a word means and having heard that word) will obviously impact overall reading comprehension.

The approach discussed in this book, Dialogic Reading with Integrated Vocabulary Enrichment (DRIVE), does not address all of the elements discussed. While the focus of DRIVE is on comprehension and vocabulary, because of the interwoven and reciprocal relationships of all the skills necessary for reading, DRIVE is offered as another powerful tool to aid the development of skilled reading.

NOTES

1. Philip Gough and William Tunmer. "Decoding, Reading, and Reading Disability." *Remedial and Special Education* 7, no. 1 (1986): 6–10.

2. National Early Literacy Panel. *Developing Early Literacy: Report of the National Early Literacy Panel* (Washington, DC: National Institute for Literacy, 2008).

3. National Reading Panel (U.S.). *Report of the National Reading Panel: Teaching Children To Read: An Evidence-Based Assessment of the Scientific Research Literature on Reading and Its Implications for Reading Instruction : Reports of the Subgroups* (Washington, DC: National Institute of Child Health and Human Development, National Institutes of Health, 2000).

4. Hollis Scarborough. "Early Identifcation of Children At Risk for Reading Disabilities: Phonological Awareness and Some Other Promising Predictors." In *Specific Reading Disability: A View of the Spectrum*, ed. Bruce Shapiro, Pasquale Accardo, and Arnold Caputo (Timonium, MD: York Press, 1998).

5. Shayne B. Piasta, Yaacov Petscher, and Laura M. Justice. "How Many Letters Should Preschoolers in Public Programs Know? The Diagnostic Efficiency of Various Preschool Letter-Naming Benchmarks for Predicting First-Grade Literacy Achievement." *Journal of Educational Psychology* 104, no. 4 (2012): 945–58. doi: 10.1037/a0027757.

6. Joseph Torgesen and Patricia Mathes. *A Basic Guide to Understanding, Assessing, and Teaching Phonological Awareness* (Austin, TX: Pro-Ed, 2000).

7. Johannes Ziegler and Usha Goswami. "Reading Acquisition, Developmental Dyslexia, and Skilled Reading across Languages: A Psycholinguistic Grain Size Theory." *Psychological Bulletin* 131, no. 1 (2005): 3–29. doi: 10.1037/0033-2909.131.1.3.

8. Lynette Bradley and Peter. E. Bryant. "Categorizing Sounds and Learning to Read: A Causal Connection." *Nature* 301 (1983): 419–421.

9. Lynette Bradley and Peter Bryant. *Rhyme and Reason In Reading and Spelling* (Ann Arbor, MI: University of Michigan Press, 1985).

10. Donald Shankweiler and Anne E. Fowler. "Questions People Ask about the Role of Phonological Processes in Learning to Read." *Reading and Writing* 17, no. 5 (2004): 483–515. doi: 10.1023/B:READ.0000044598.81628.e6.

11. Linnea C. Ehri "Orthographic Mapping in the Acquisition of Sight Word Reading, Spelling Memory, and Vocabulary Learning." *Scientific Studies of Reading* 18, no. 1 (2014): 5–21. doi: 10.1080/10888438.2013.819356.

12. Hollis Scarborough. "Connecting Early Language and Literacy to Later Reading (Dis)abilities." In *Handbook for Research in Early Literacy*, ed. Susan Neuman and David Dickisnon (New York: Guilford Press, 2001), 97–110.

13. Linnea C. Ehri, Simone R. Nunes, Steven A. Stahl, and Dale M. Willows. "Systematic Phonics Instruction Helps Students Learn to Read: Evidence from the National Reading Panel's Meta-Analysis." *Review of Educational Research* 71, no. 3 (2001): 393–447. doi: 10.3102/00346543071003393.

14. Ibid.

15. Lynn Fuchs, Douglas Fuchs, Michelle K Hosp, and Joseph R Jenkins. "Oral Reading Fluency as an Indicator of Reading Competence: A Theoretical, Empirical, and Historical Analysis," *Scientific Studies of Reading* 5, no. 3 (2001): 239–256.

16. Elizabeth Stevens, Melodee A Walker, and Sharon Vaughn. "The Effects of Reading Fluency Interventions on the Reading Fluency and Reading Comprehension Performance of Elementary Students With Learning Disabilities: A Synthesis of the Research from 2001 to 2014." *Journal of Learning Disabilities* 50, no. 5 (2017): 576–90. doi: 10.1177/0022219416638028.

17. David Chard, Sharon Vaughn, and Brenda-Jean Tyler. "A Synthesis of Research on Effective Interventions for Building Reading Fluency with Elementary Students with Learning Disabilities." *Journal of Learning Disabilities* 35, no. 5 (2002): 386–406.

18. Gene P. Ouellette. "What's Meaning Got to Do with It: The Role of Vocabulary in Word Reading and Reading Comprehension." *Journal of Educational Psychology* 98, no. 3 (2006): 554–66.

19. Scarborough, "Early Identifcation of Children At Risk for Reading Disabilities: Phonological Awareness and Some Other Promising Predictors."

20. Ouellette, "What's Meaning Got to Do with It: The Role of Vocabulary in Word Reading and Reading Comprehension."

21. Erika Hoff. "The Specificity of Environmental Influence: Socioeconomic Status Affects Early Vocabulary Development via Maternal Speech." *Child Development* 74, no. 5 (2003): 1368–78. doi: 10.1111/1467-8624.00612.

22. Adriana Weisleder and Anne Fernald. "Talking to Children Matters: Early Language Experience Strengthens Processing and Builds Vocabulary." *Psychological Science* 24, no. 11 (2013): 2143–52. doi: 10.1177/0956797613488145.

23. Evelyn Ford-Connors and Jeanne R. Paratore. "Vocabulary Instruction in Fifth Grade and Beyond: Sources of Word Learning and Productive Contexts for Development." *Review of Educational Research* 85, no. 1 (2015): 50–91.

24. National Reading Panel, *Report of the National Reading Panel: Teaching Children To Read : An Evidence-Based Assessment of the Scientific Research Literature on Reading and Its Implications for Reading Instruction.*

25. Fiona Duff and Paula Clarke. "Practitioner Review: Reading Disorders: What Are the Effective Interventions and How Should They Be Implemented and Evaluated?" *Journal of Child Psychology and Psychiatry* 52 (2011): 3–12. doi: 10.1111/j.1469-7610.2010.02310.x.

26. Charles Hulme and Margaret Snowling. "Children's Reading Comprehension Difficulties: Nature, Causes, and Treatments." *Current Directions in Psychological Science* 20, no. 3 (2011): 139–142. doi: 10.1177/0963721411408673.

27. Natalie Wexler. *The Knowledge Gap* (New York: Avery, 2019).

28. William Nagy and Judith Scott. "Vocabulary Processes." In *Handbook of Reading Research*, ed. Michael Kamil, Peter Mosenthal, P. David Pearson, and Rebecca Barr (Mahwah, NJ: Erlbaum, 2000), 269–284.

29. Keith Stanovich. "Matthew Effects in Reading: Some Consequences of Individual Differences in the Acquisition of Literacy." *Reading Research Quarterly* 21 no. 4 (1986): 360–407.

30. William Nagy and Richard C. Anderson. "How Many Words Are There in Printed School English?" *Reading Research Quarterly* 19, no. 3 (1984): 304–30. doi: 10.2307/747823.

Chapter 2

What Is the DRIVE Approach?

Dialogic Reading with Integrated Vocabulary Enrichment, or DRIVE, is a user-friendly shared book reading approach based on research that is designed to promote both vocabulary development and reading comprehension in young readers. This chapter will:

- provide an overview of the approach and introduce the techniques (also called strategies) that are part of the approach, which will be discussed in more detail in subsequent chapters;
- highlight some of the research that led to the development of DRIVE as well as supporting evidence for this approach.

It is important to note here that the use of DRIVE alone will not teach a child to read, nor will it ensure that they will necessarily become proficient readers. However, together with a foundation of the other key elements that are discussed in chapter 1, DRIVE can be a powerful addition to promoting literacy for many young children.

DIALOGIC READING WITH INTEGRATED VOCABULARY ENRICHMENT (DRIVE)

DRIVE was developed based on a shared book reading approach called dialogic reading that was created by researcher Grover Whitehurst and colleagues.[1,2,3] This original dialogic reading approach was developed for parents, caregivers, and childcare teachers to use with children from ages two through five.[4]

During shared book reading, adults stop frequently to ask open-ended questions, not in an evaluative way such as asking a question and expecting a correct answer, but in a conversational way that encourages development of conversational turn-taking, vocabulary, expressive language, and comprehension. Adults encourage dialogue by asking questions using five types of question prompts summarized by the acronym CROWD: completion (fill-in-the-blank), recall questions, open-ended questions, wh-questions (what, where, why), and distancing questions (making personal connections to the story).

Adults also engage in behaviors while reading which are summarized by the acronym, PEER. They prompt the child to label objects or talk about the story. They evaluate the child's responses (which refers to giving praise and encouragement). Adults also expand on the child's incomplete responses and encourage them to repeat the modeled responses.

In more recent research with schools in high-poverty areas, the authors of this book used dialogic reading as an intervention for kindergarten through second-grade students who were at risk for developing reading problems. Many of these children had typical knowledge about print, phonological skills, word recognition, and decoding skills (all discussed in chapter 1). But they performed below grade level on vocabulary and comprehension.[5] Teachers also noted that children had limited background knowledge about common events in stories, which is necessary to support vocabulary development and comprehension.

The original research by Whitehurst and colleagues found that dialogic reading was beneficial for improving children's vocabulary and language comprehension. So, this approach was chosen to address these weaknesses that were found in kindergarten through second-grade children who were struggling with reading. The authors of this book adapted the original approach in two important ways so that it would be more appropriate to use with these early elementary-age readers.

First, the number of techniques (also called strategies or prompts) was streamlined. The completion prompt in the original CROWD acronym was eliminated because it encourages one-word responses ("Sal went to pick . . ."). The recall prompt in the PEER acronym was eliminated because it is redundant with Wh-questions which can be used to ask the child to recall the story ("What happened in the story last time?"). The new approach developed by the authors of this book is summarized as a single acronym, EMPOWERED (explained in the next section and in more detail in chapter 3).

A second improvement on the original dialogic reading approach involved encouraging vocabulary using some of the EMPOWERED techniques (explained in more detail in chapter 4). None of the research studies on dialogic reading focused on identifying and discussing important vocabulary words while reading.[6] Yet, vocabulary knowledge helps foster children's reading comprehension and is a robust predictor of later reading success.[7,8] Therefore, taking time to discuss the meaning of vocabulary words can improve children's understanding of the story and enhance their overall reading comprehension.

With these two adaptations of dialogic reading—streamlining the techniques that adults use into an easy-to-remember acronym, EMPOWERED, and emphasizing the importance of discussing vocabulary in stories—the new dialogic reading approach can be used with students in the primary grades as well as with younger, preschool-age children. This new approach is called Dialogic Reading with Integrated Vocabulary Enrichment, or DRIVE. Next, you will learn more about how to use the EMPOWERED strategies during reading sessions.

EMPOWERED TECHNIQUES

Table 2.1 shows the EMPOWERED techniques used in the DRIVE approach along with examples of each technique. Here, readers have a brief introduction to each of the strategies comprising the DRIVE approach, which are discussed further in chapters 3 and 4.

First, the E-M in the acronym refers to Encouraging vocabulary and Making reading fun. Making the reading activity fun and engaging was a recommendation from the researchers who created the original dialogic reading approach.[9] Likewise, making the reading experience enjoyable has always been a part of the DRIVE approach. It was formally added to the M in the acronym to create an explicit reminder for the reader. The strategy of making the reading session fun will be covered in greater detail in chapter 6 "Tips to Consider while Reading."

Table 2.1 Dialogic Reading with Integrated Vocabulary Enrichment (DRIVE) Techniques

Technique		Example
*E*ncourage Vocabulary	Discuss what vocabulary words mean within the story using Wh-questions, expansion, encouraging repetition, and evaluation techniques.	• Adult: What do you think *gaze* means? • Child: (shrugs shoulders) • Adult: "Do we gaze with our ears (tugging ears) or our eyes (using binocular mime)?" • Child: "Our eyes!" • Adult: "So, what do we do when we gaze?" • Child: "We look with our eyes."
*M*ake It Fun	Have fun reading and keep the dialogue light and engaging.	• Use an upbeat tone of voice • Use mime and movements • Do not coerce children to read if they are disinterested, fatigued, etc.
*P*rompt Frequently	Prompt the child to identify vocabulary in the story and talk about the story and its characters.	• "What does this word mean?" • "Tell me what's going on here."
*O*pen-Ended Questions	Encourage children to respond in their own words using more than a one-word answer.	• "What's happening in the story?" (a good way to prompt recall when reading extends over multiple sessions) • "Why do you think she's unhappy?" • "What will happen next?" • "How would you feel if you were (the character)?"
*W*h-Questions	What, where, and why questions.	• "What do you think will happen next?" • "Why did Jack stay home from school?" • "Where do you think the family is going?"
*E*xpand the Child's Responses	Model slightly more advanced language by repeating what the child says, but with a bit more information or in a more advanced form.	• Adult: "Do you have a hobby, something you like to do in your free time?" • Child: "basketball." • Adult: "Oh, so your hobby is playing basketball."

(*Continued*)

Table 2.1 Continued

Technique		Example
Encourage **R**epetition	Encourage the child to repeat the expanded utterance.	• Adult: "Alphonse found a treasure chest deep in the ocean. What would you do with buried treasure?" • Child: "Buy candy." • Adult: "Oh, so you would buy candy with the buried treasure. Now you tell me: 'I would buy candy with the treasure.'"
Evaluate the Child's Responses	Praise the child's correct responses and gently offer alternative labels or answers for incorrect responses.	• Adult (asking about the cover picture): "What animal is that?" • Child: "A dog." • Adult: "Well, the title of the story is *The Wolf's Chicken Stew* and he's holding a cookbook, so I'll bet that's a wolf."
Distancing Prompts	Ask questions that involve personal connections of the book to the child's own life.	• "Louis' mom didn't want him to keep the frog as a pet. Do you have any pets?" • "Antonio's granny made him a big bag of jam sandwiches. What do you like to eat for lunch?"

So, how do you **E**ncourage vocabulary, and which words should you focus on? It is best to choose words that (1) are interesting or useful, (2) will help with the overall comprehension of the story, and (3) you can define or explain in a way that children will understand.[10,11] For example, in *Sylvester and the Magic Pebble* by William Steig, the word *remarkable* refers to the pebble that Sylvester has found. This word is interesting, and it is helpful for children to know the meaning of it to advance their understanding of the story. It is also relatively easy to explain to children.

Words, such as *remarkable*, are what researcher Isabel Beck and colleagues consider "Tier 2" words. These are words that are not very common in everyday language but are learned through interaction with text and are often useful across a variety of contexts.[12] Here, the pebble is remarkable because it has magic powers, but remarkable can be used to describe so many other objects or experiences children will have.

The aim is not for children to provide a dictionary definition, but to help them develop their own understanding of the word in the context of the story. Children need to use a new word many times and in multiple contexts in order to incorporate it into their vocabulary.[13,14] To do this, adults can use scaffolding, which is any support that will help children provide an appropriate response.[15] Some examples of scaffolds are hints, clues, modifying the question, or re-reading.

Another way to scaffold children's understanding of new vocabulary in stories is through mime. Encourage the child to mime a word if they do not initially know how to explain it. For example, for *stomping*, ask them to show you this action (or you can show them first and have them imitate the action). Then, ask the child to use words to describe what they did. Children find the use of mimes or actions to be very amusing. Therefore, this scaffold also qualifies as part of the technique, Make it fun.

Next, the P-O-W in the acronym refers to behaviors of the adult reader—Prompt frequently using Open-ended questions and Wh-questions. The Prompt frequently strategy reminds the adult to take time to stop and ask questions about the story, which will be explained in more detail in chapter 3. Prompting begins with the cover of the book. By beginning with the cover, you are helping the child to activate any prior knowledge that they may have about the story to aid comprehension. Prompting by starting with the cover can be done by:

- asking open-ended Wh-questions such as who are the people on the cover or what do you think is going to happen in this story (a prediction question); or
- asking personal connection questions about the topic (referred to as Distancing prompts, discussed later in the chapter).

Open-ended questions result in more than a one-word answer, typically have many possible responses, and often take the form of a Wh-question (what, where, why), as shown in table 2.1. Open-ended and Wh-questions can be used to:

- ask about the characters, their feelings, the plot, predictions about what will happen next, and recalling earlier parts of the story; and
- identify new vocabulary words and discuss their meaning, the E (Encourage vocabulary) in EMPOWERED.

Asking open-ended questions is an effective strategy for encouraging students to provide more than a one-word answer.[16]

However, when children do provide only a one-word response or an incomplete phrase, the adult reader needs to use the next two techniques, the E-R in EMPOWERED, namely Expand on the child's response and encourage the child to Repeat your expansion.

- Expanding on the child's one-word answer or incomplete response models more complex language and is consistent with typical practices of parents when speaking with their children.[17,18]
- Encouraging the child to repeat the expanded utterance allows the child to take ownership of these new language forms.

Research has found that Expanding and encouraging Repetition tend to be the most challenging techniques to use while reading with a child.[19] However, these are essential to developing more advanced oral language. Chapter 3 discusses ways that adults can become more comfortable with these strategies.

The next EMPOWERED technique is to Evaluate the child's responses, which refers to providing praise and encouragement. The term "evaluation" was used in the PEER acronym of the original dialogic reading approach developed by Whitehurst and colleagues.[20] So, it has been retained in the EMPOWERED acronym of the DRIVE approach.

As an example of the "Expand-encourage Repetition-Evaluate" sequence in the EMPOWERED acronym, consider the previous example of the child learning the meaning of *stomping*. The child may say, "Stomping is banging your feet like this [performing the action] to make noise." The adult might respond, "Oh, so stomping is moving your feet up and down heavily to make noise" (Expansion). "Now you tell me what stomping is" (encourage Repetition). Once the child provides a more elaborated response, the adult praises the child's efforts, as in "That's a great way to explain *stomping*!" (Evaluation).

Finally, the D in EMPOWERED refers to Distancing prompts, a type of prompt in the original CROWD acronym that refers to personal connection questions.[21] For example, in *Blueberries for Sal* by Robert McCloskey, we might ask "Have you ever been blueberry picking?" or "What types of activities do you like to do with your family?" Personal connection questions encourage children to use vocabulary, formulate more complex language, and activate prior knowledge that may be relevant to story comprehension.

BENEFITS OF DIALOGIC READING WITH INTEGRATED VOCABULARY ENRICHMENT (DRIVE)

As discussed in the preface, DRIVE is an evidence-based reading intervention. In studies on the original dialogic reading approach, researchers taught middle-class parents and day-care teachers who were working with children from high-poverty backgrounds to use dialogic reading. Results indicated that using the approach for about six weeks facilitated the development of preschool children's vocabulary and language skills.[22,23]

The authors of this book have conducted research on DRIVE with students from kindergarten through second grade. Studies have shown that students with below grade-level comprehension can improve this ability by participating in one-on-one DRIVE intervention sessions of about ten minutes each over a period of six to twelve weeks.

- In one study, first-grade students with very poor reading comprehension who received DRIVE along with their school's intervention significantly improved over this short period, narrowing the gap with their typically achieving peers.
- By comparison, students who received *only* their school's intervention showed a decline in comprehension performance over the same period.[24]

This pattern of results was obtained again in subsequent research studies. Second graders in an urban school who had below grade-level reading comprehension received three hours of DRIVE intervention (ten-minute individual sessions spaced over twelve weeks) and showed improvement that narrowed the gap with typically achieving students. Research with struggling first-grade readers in an urban public school in two consecutive school years again showed that about four hours of DRIVE (in ten-minute sessions) narrowed the gap in reading comprehension between these struggling readers and typically achieving peers.[25]

Similar results were found in a case study of five kindergarteners in an urban public school who had below-average oral language comprehension. Children received a total of about ninety minutes of the DRIVE intervention in ten-minute sessions over six weeks, which was slightly less than the typical two hours of intervention in previous research with first and second graders. All five of these kindergarteners improved their language comprehension to average performance (which means typical for their age), narrowing the gap with their classmates who already had average language comprehension performance.[26]

The DRIVE approach also can yield positive effects on the attitudes and reading motivation of at-risk early readers. After only six to eight weeks of reading individually with children in schools using DRIVE, it was amazing to see children, who did not like reading and who were hesitant to engage in dialogue, become excited about reading. Undergraduate students who implemented the intervention would enter the classroom, and children would exclaim "Pick me!"

Also, toward the end of the intervention some children had taken such ownership of the dialogic process that they wanted to ask their own questions to the adults as they read a story. Survey data on children's attitudes about the intervention show that about 83 percent of first graders and 82 percent of second graders who received the DRIVE intervention reported feeling happy about participating in this reading approach.[27]

SUMMARY

DRIVE is a user-friendly approach for supporting the language and reading development of early elementary readers and is especially powerful for children who may start school with less print exposure and home reading experience. Because DRIVE is not a commercial curriculum, it is a cost-effective approach that can be used by parents, educators, and librarians to supplement the school's literacy instruction and formal intervention services. Reading with children using DRIVE for a few minutes each day can be a simple way to promote comprehension and vocabulary development while encouraging children to develop a positive attitude about reading.

NOTES

1. Grover J. Whitehurst, David S. Arnold, Jeffery N. Epstein, Andrea L. Angell, Meagan Smith, and Janet E. Fischel. "A Picture Book Reading

Intervention in Day Care and Home for Children from Low-Income Families." *Developmental Psychology* 30, no. 5 (1994): 679–689.

2. Grover J. Whitehurst, Francine L. Falco, Christopher J. Lonigan, Janet E. Fischel, Barbara D. DeBaryshe, Marta C. Valdez-Menchaca, and Marie Caulfield. "Accelerating Language Development through Picture Book Reading." *Developmental Psychology* 24, no. 4 (1988): 552–559.

3. Grover J. Whitehurst, Deane A. Crone, Andrea A. Zevenbergen, Margaret D. Schultz, Olivia N. Velting, and Janet E. Fischel. "Outcomes of an Emergent Literacy Intervention from Head Start through Second Grade." *Journal of Educational Psychology* 91, no. 2 (1999): 261–272.

4. Andrea Zevenbergen and Grover Whitehurst. "Dialogic Reading: A Shared Picture Book Intervention for Preschoolers." In *On Reading Books to Children: Parents and Teachers*, ed. Anne van Kleek, Steven Stahl and Eurydice Bauer (Mahwah, NJ: Lawrence Erlbaum Associates, 2003), 177–220.

5. Cheryl Durwin, Deborah Carroll, and Dina Moore. "Dialogic Reading: A Theory-Based Approach to Early Reading Intervention in Urban Schools" (Poster presented at the annual meeting of the Eastern Psychological Association, New York, March 2016).

6. Barbara A. Wasik, Annemarie H. Hindman, and Emily K. Snell. "Book Reading and Vocabulary Development: A Systematic Review." *Early Childhood Research Quarterly* 37 (2016): 39–57. doi: 10.1016/j.ecresq.2016.04.003.

7. Cor Aarnoutse and Jan van Leeuwe. "Relation Between Reading Comprehension, Vocabulary, Reading Pleasure, and Reading Frequency." *Educational Research and Evaluation* 4, no. 2 (1998): 143–166. doi: 10.1076/edre.4.2.143.6960.

8. Ludo Verhoeven, Jan van Leeuwe, and Anne Vermeer. "Vocabulary Growth and Reading Development across the Elementary School Years." *Scientific Studies of Reading* 15, no. 1 (2011): 8–25.

9. David H. Arnold, Christopher J. Lonigan, Grover J. Whitehurst, and Jeffery N. Epstein. "Accelerating Language Development Through Picture Book Reading: Replication and Extension to a Videotape Training Format." *Journal of Educational Psychology* 86, no. 2 (1994): 235–243.

10. Isabel Beck, Margaret McKeown, and Linda Kucan. *Bringing Words to Life: Robust Vocabulary Instruction* (New York: Guilford Press, 2002).

11. Isabel Beck, Margaret McKeown, and Linda Kucan. *Bringing Words to Life: Robust Vocabulary Instruction*, 2nd ed. (New York: Guilford Press, 2013).

12. Margaret G. McKeown "Effective Vocabulary Instruction Fosters Knowing Words, Using Words, and Understanding How Words Work." *Language, Speech, and Hearing Services in Schools* 50, no. 4 (2019): 466–476. doi: 10.1044/2019_LSHSS-VOIA-18-0126.

13. Andrew Biemiller. "Teaching Vocabulary: Early, Direct, and Sequential." *American Educator* 25 (2001, Spring): 24–28, 47.

14. Susan Goldin-Meadow, Susan C. Levine, Larry V. Hedges, Janellen Huttenlocher, Stephen W. Raudenbush, and Steven L. Small. "New Evidence about Language and Cognitive Development Based on a Longitudinal Study: Hypotheses for Intervention." *American Psychologist* 69, no. 6 (2014): 588–599.

15. David Wood, Jerome S. Bruner, and Gail Ross. "The Role of Tutoring in Problem Solving." *Journal of Child Psychology & Psychiatry* 17 (1976): 89–100.

16. Barbara A. Wasik and Annemarie H. Hindman. "Realizing the Promise of Open-Ended Questions." *The Reading Teacher* 67, no. 4 (2013): 302–311. doi: 10.1002/trtr.1218.

17. Penny Levickis, Sheena Reilly, Luigi Girolametto, Obioha C. Ukoumunne, and Melissa Wake. "Maternal Behaviors Promoting Language Acquisition in Slow-to-Talk Toddlers." *Journal of Developmental & Behavioral Pediatrics* 35, no. 4 (May 2014): 274–281. doi: 10.1097/DBP.0000000000000056.

18. Catherine S. Tamis-LeMonda, Marc H. Bornstein, and Lisa Baumwell. "Maternal Responsiveness and Children's Achievement of Language Milestones." *Child Development* 72, no. 3 (2001): 748–767. doi: 10.1111/1467-8624.00313.

19. Brianna Chiaraluce. "Evaluating the Treatment Fidelity of a Dialogic Reading Intervention." (Poster presented at the annual meeting of the Northeastern Educational Research Association, Trumbull, CT, October 2018).

20. Jessica Blom-Hoffman, Therese M. O'Neil-Pirozzi, and Joanna Cutting. "Read Together, Talk Together: The Acceptability of Teaching Parents to Use Dialogic Reading Strategies via Videotaped Instruction." *Psychology in the Schools* 43, no. 1 (2006): 71–78.

21. Zevenbergen and Whitehurst. "Dialogic Reading: A Shared Picture Book Intervention for Preschoolers."

22. Christopher J. Lonigan and Grover J. Whitehurst. 1998. "Relative Efficacy of Parent and Teacher Involvement in a Shared-Reading Intervention for Preschool Children from Low-Income Backgrounds." *Early Childhood Research Quarterly* 13, no. 2 (1998): 263–290.

23. Marta C. Valdez-Menchaca, and Grover J. Whitehurst. "Accelerating Language Development Through Picture Book Reading: A Systematic Extension to Mexican Day Care." *Developmental Psychology* 28, no. 6 (1992): 1106–1114.

24. Durwin et al., "Dialogic Reading: A Theory-Based Approach to Early Reading Intervention in Urban Schools."

25. Cheryl Durwin, Dina Moore, Deborah Carroll, and Brianna Chiaraluce. "Efficacy of a Dialogic Reading Intervention for At-Risk Readers in Urban

Schools" (Paper presented at the annual meeting of the American Educational Research Association, New York, April 2018).

26. Cheryl Durwin, Dina Moore, and Deborah Carroll. "Can a Brief Dialogic Reading Intervention Improve Listening Comprehension of At-Risk Kindergartners?" (Paper at roundtable session of annual meeting of the American Educational Research Association, San Francisco, CA, April 2020. Conference Canceled). http://tinyurl.com/v6gx3dh.

27. Durwin et al., "Efficacy of a Dialogic Reading Intervention for At-Risk Readers in Urban Schools."

Chapter 3

Overview of EMPOWERED Strategies

In this chapter, you will see how the EMPOWERED strategies discussed in chapter 2 are used together in the context of reading a story. Excerpts from two stories will be used throughout the chapter. One is *Hello Lighthouse* by Sophie Blackall (shown in Textbox 3.1), which is ideal for younger, preschool-age children but could also be used with elementary-age children if the reader has only a short amount of time. The other is *The Patchwork Quilt* by Valerie Flournoy (shown in Textbox 3.2), which is a longer book that will require multiple reading sessions to finish and is therefore more appropriate for elementary-age readers.

START WITH THE COVER

Start your reading session by using the book cover. Read the title of the story and identify the author. Ask the child to tell you what they think the story is about using the title and picture on the cover. This is not a situation in which there is a correct or incorrect answer. The emphasis is on making a prediction about the story based on this information, then finding out what actually happens as the adult and child read.

Adults also can ask questions about words in the title or objects in the cover picture to establish necessary background knowledge that is important for story comprehension. For example, in the *Hello Lighthouse* dialogue shown in Textbox 3.1, the adult asks the child if they know the purpose of a lighthouse (<u>W</u>h-question). The adult then follows with a <u>D</u>istancing question, asking the child if they have seen a lighthouse. In this case, the child has seen a lighthouse. If a child did not have this prior knowledge, the dialogue would involve explaining the purpose of a lighthouse. Background knowledge about a lighthouse is important to establish before reading because the lighthouse and its keeper are the focus of the story.

TEXTBOX 3.1: SAMPLE DIALOGUE FROM A DRIVE READING SESSION USING *HELLO LIGHTHOUSE* BY SOPHIE BLACKALL

Adult: (showing cover) This book is called *Hello Lighthouse* by Sophie Blackall. Do you know what a lighthouse is for? (<u>W</u>h-question).
Child: I saw a lighthouse at the beach!
Adult: You were at the beach and saw a lighthouse? Did you get to go inside the lighthouse? (<u>E</u>xpansion; <u>D</u>istancing)
Child: Yes, we went inside and saw the light.
Adult: And what does the light do in the lighthouse? (<u>W</u>h-question).
Child: Keeps boats from crashing.
Adult: That's right the lighthouse shines a light and shows ships where the rocks are. (<u>E</u>xpansion) Now remind me, what does the light do in the lighthouse? (<u>R</u>epetition)
Child: It shines light so you can see where the rocks are.
Adult: That's right. (<u>E</u>valuation). Let's start reading.

Skipping ahead a few pages:

Text: "The new keeper arrives to replace the old, to carry on tending the light."
Adult: Do you know what tending means? (<u>W</u>h-question; <u>E</u>ncourage vocabulary)
Child: I think it means he fixes the light.
Adult: That's close. Tending means taking care of. The keeper takes care of the light so that it is always shining for the ships.

Now, can you say what tending means? (Expansion and encourage Repetition)
Child: Tending means he takes care of the light.
Adult: Great! Let's read some more. (Evaluation)

Skipping ahead a few pages:

Text: "The keeper boils water and drinks his tea, as he fishes for cod from the window. He sets the table and hums a tune and wishes for someone to talk to."
Adult: Why do you think the keeper wishes for someone to talk to? (Wh-question)
Child: Because he's by himself.
Adult: Yes, that's true (Evaluation). He is by himself. How do you think he feels (Open-ended)?
Child: Sad.
Adult: I think he's feeling sad, too, because he is lonely and doesn't have anyone to talk to. (Expansion) Have you ever felt lonely? (Distancing prompt)
Child: When I didn't have anyone to play with at recess today.
Adult: It does feel lonely to not have anyone to play with at recess. Remind me, what does lonely mean? (Repetition)
Child: It means you're alone and you want to be with people.
Adult: That's right! (Evaluation). Let's keep reading.

Similarly, in *The Patchwork Quilt* it is important to know what the words *patchwork* and *quilt* mean in order to comprehend the story. In the dialogue shown in textbox 3.2, the adult asks the child who the people illustrated on the cover might be (Wh-question) and continues with a question about the quilt. Some children will associate the word *quilt* with a blanket, but most will not know what *patchwork* means. The word *patchwork* appears often throughout the book, allowing multiple opportunities for the child to construct their own meaning of the word (as discussed in chapter 2). Therefore, it is critical to establish an initial understanding of *patchwork* which will become more deeply understood as the story progresses.

TEXTBOX 3.2: SAMPLE DIALOGUE FROM A DRIVE READING SESSION USING *THE PATCHWORK QUILT* BY VALERIE FLOURNOY

Adult: (showing cover): This book is called *The Patchwork Quilt* by Valerie Flournoy. Who do you think these people are on the cover? (Wh-question).
Child: An old lady and a girl.
Adult: Yes, that's right. (Evaluation). I wonder if the lady is a grandmother and that is her granddaughter. We'll find out as we read. (Expansion). Do you know what this is (pointing to the quilt)? (Wh-question).
Child: A blanket.
Adult: Yes. This kind of blanket called a quilt. It's a special kind called a patchwork quilt. See the squares? These are pieces of fabric, and when you put them together, they'll become a patchwork quilt. So, what is this blanket called? (Wh-question).
Child: It's a patchwork quilt.
Adult: Right! (Evaluation). Let's begin reading the story.

First page:

Text: "Tanya sat restlessly on her chair at the kitchen window.... She was anxious to go outside and enjoy the fresh air and the arrival of spring."
Adult: Do you know what anxious means? (Wh-question; Encourage vocabulary)
Child: Scared.
Adult: That's close. Sometimes anxious means worried. But here Tanya is anxious to go outside. (Evaluation). Do you think she *really, really* wants to go outside?
Child: Yes!
Adult: So, anxious means you want to do something very, very much and can't wait to do it. Now remind me, what does anxious mean? (Repetition).
Child: Anxious means you can't wait to do something.
Adult: That's a great way to explain anxious! (Evaluation)

Skipping ahead a few pages:

Text: "It's gonna take quite a while to make this quilt, not a couple days or a week—not even a month. A good quilt, a masterpiece . . ."
Adult: Grandma calls the quilt a masterpiece. What is a masterpiece? (Wh-question).
Child: I don't know.
Adult: Have you ever made a drawing or art project at school and your teacher thought it was excellent and so very beautiful? Maybe you put it on the refrigerator for everyone to see? (Distancing)
Child: Yes, I painted a picture of a giraffe and mommy put it on the refrigerator.
Adult: So, you painted a masterpiece. A masterpiece is something you make or build that is very beautiful and unique, a one-of-a-kind. Now you tell me, what is a masterpiece? (Repetition).
Child: It's like my painting that's something very special.
Adult: Yes, it's something you make that's very special and everyone loves it. (Evaluation and Expansion).

Skipping ahead a few pages:

Text: ". . . Grandma was telling Mama all about quilts and how *this* quilt would be very special . . . , then she saw Mama pick up a piece of fabric, rub it with her fingers, and smile."
Adult: (ending the reading session for the day). What do you think is going to happen next? (Wh-question, Open-ended question).
Child: Mama's going to help with the quilt.
Adult: That's a really good prediction. (Evaluation). We'll see what happens when we read next time.

ENCOURAGE VOCABULARY AND MAKE IT FUN

The first two strategies in the EMPOWERED acronym that were introduced in chapter 2 are Encourage vocabulary and Make it fun. Encouraging vocabulary is discussed in greater detail in chapter 4 where the reader will learn about the importance of vocabulary for reading comprehension, how to choose appropriate words for a reading session, and how to use some of the other EMPOWERED strategies to prompt discussion of the vocabulary words in the story. In this chapter, the Encourage vocabulary strategy is illustrated in:

- Textbox 3.1 when the adult asks the child about the word *tending* in *Hello Lighthouse*, and
- Textbox 3.2 when the adult asks about the meaning of *anxious* and *masterpiece* in *The Patchwork Quilt*.

The strategy Make it fun will be discussed in greater detail in chapter 6 "Tips to Consider while Reading." One general suggestion while reading is to make sure that you *sound* like you are enthusiastic and excited to read the story. In reading, this refers to the idea of using the proper prosody, or appropriate rhythm, tone, pitch, pauses, stress, and emotion for the content you are reading. This does not mean that you have to act out voices or read in a way that is not comfortable for you, but be mindful of the tone of your voice and take your time to enjoy the story.

In Textbox 3.2 showing *The Patchwork Quilt* dialogue, you see a glimpse of one strategy for making reading fun, which is to use an upbeat, exaggerated tone of voice. When the adult asks the child about the character Tanya being anxious to go outside by saying, "Do you think she *really, really* wants to go outside?" you can imagine a change in the adult's tone of voice when emphasizing the words *really, really* and perhaps a facial expression that indicates someone who is very eager to do something.

Another way to make the reading experience fun is to use mime and movements. For example, when introducing the word *restlessly* in *The Patchwork Quilt*, the adult might first provide a hint to the child that a person who is restless is very wiggly, and then would ask the child to demonstrate wiggly. Children are typically very eager to mime words and generate movements. Moving around is generally discouraged during reading sessions, especially in a structured setting such as schools. This is a refreshing change of pace for children, it encourages them to be active, and makes it fun.

PROMPT FREQUENTLY

The Prompt frequently strategy is a reminder for the adult to create multiple opportunities for conversations with the child about the story.

Stopping frequently to discuss the story may be very different from what you might typically do when reading with a child, and it may even feel a bit strange at first. However, this is an essential component of dialogic reading. The process of continually stopping to discuss and reflect on the story encourages children to actively construct an understanding of the characters' actions and emotions and the events that unfold rather than passively listening to the story.

You might be wondering how many prompts are enough? Some experts recommend one or two prompts per page.[1] The number of prompts will actually depend on the amount of text appearing on a page that could provide useful information for discussion, as well as characteristics of the child such as age, interest level, and attention span.

Where to stop on a page will also depend on these factors. For a book that has very little text on a page, such as *The Little House* by Virginia Lee Burton or *Doctor De Soto* by William Steig, it is a good idea to read the entire text and then begin the dialogue. For books, such as *The Patchwork Quilt* by Valerie Flournoy or *The Enormous Crocodile* by Roald Dahl, that contain several para-graphs of text on a page, remember these rules of thumb:

- always finish a paragraph rather than stopping in the middle to ask a question; and
- look for places where it seems natural to stop so that you do not interrupt the flow of the story.

If you decide to read an entire page or several paragraphs at once, a good idea might be to use a cue such as "Now, let's go back and talk about what we've read." To refresh the reader's memory as you discuss, you can also re-read a sentence, especially if introducing a vocabulary word.

Some creators of the original dialogic reading approach also recommend that adults continue to follow up children's responses with additional questions until there is no more to say about a page.[2] For many children, especially younger ones and those who are not accustomed to being asked questions, this will seem excessive. A few prompts per page is typically all that is needed. If the child is getting bored or frustrated by the questioning, just read a few pages without stopping to ask questions.[3]

There is no single rule for the ideal number of questions to ask. There is also no standard principle for where to stop on a page. Use your best judgment along with the guidelines discussed here, and take your cues from the child.

OPEN-ENDED QUESTIONS AND WH-QUESTIONS

When prompting frequently, the aim is to use questions that encourage the child to give more than a one-word answer.[4] To do this, use Open-ended questions rather than closed-ended questions. For example, in the dialogue about the cover of *The Patchwork Quilt*, which shows Tanya and her grandmother, the adult asks, "Who do you think these people are on the cover?" This is an example of an Open-ended question, as contrasted with a question such as "Is that a girl on the cover?" which yields a yes or no answer.

In the *Hello Lighthouse* dialogue, the adult asks "How do you think he feels?" referring to the lighthouse keeper. This is an Open-ended question because there are many possible answers, such as sad, lonely, or isolated. The child happened to respond with one word (sad). The adult replied with an Expansion to model a more elaborate response to an open-ended question and followed up with a Distancing prompt.

If the adult had asked, "Do you think he feels sad?" this would be an example of a closed-ended question which only requires a one-word response, in this case *yes* or *no*. Remember that in dialogic reading, try to use Open-ended questions whenever possible because these types of questions will encourage children to formulate more complex language.

Imagine that when the adult asked the child about how the lighthouse keeper felt, the child replied "I don't know." It is common for children to respond that they do not know or even to shrug their shoulders. In this case, the adult can use other EMPOWERED strategies to encourage the child to respond. For example, the adult might use their own personal connection (Distancing) to model a response, saying "If I were alone in the lighthouse, I would feel sad. How about you?"

Adults also can use Wh-questions, which are questions that start with *who*, *what*, *where*, *when*, or *why*. These questions typically elicit more than a one-word response. For example, in the *Hello Lighthouse* dialogue, the adult asks "Why do you think the keeper wishes for someone to talk to?" This question encourages the child to understand the character's emotion and helps to advance the child's comprehension of the story. Wh-questions serve an important role as book-end questions, discussed further in chapter 6. They can be used:

- when resuming a reading session with the same book to encourage recall of the story, as in "What happened in the story last time?" and
- at the end of a session to make a prediction, as when the adult in *The Patchwork Quilt* dialogue asks, "What do you think is going to happen next?"

Notice that the previous examples of Wh-questions also count as Open-ended questions. Not all Wh-questions are open-ended, though. The researchers of the original dialogic reading approach suggested that *"what"* questions can be closed-ended, such as "What is that?" (a bear) or "What color is that?" (blue).[5] However, in the DRIVE approach it is generally recommended that adults focus on using open-ended types of Wh-questions.

There are a few instances where closed-ended questions are appropriate, such as when reading with very young children (ages 1–3) or when reading with children who are reluctant to respond to the adult's questioning. In this case, ease the child into the DRIVE process by starting with simple, closed-ended questioning and slowly progressing to Open-ended and Wh-questions as the child becomes more comfortable with the process.

EXPANSION

After the child provides a response, it is often necessary to Expand on the child's utterance to model a more advanced way to express the idea. This technique is typically used by parents in everyday conversations with young children to promote language development.[6,7] For example, a toddler may say "ball," pointing to his red plastic ball. The caregiver might reply, "Do you want your ball? Here is your ball." This expands the toddler's one-word utterance into a more elaborate and grammatically complex statement.

During a DRIVE session, adults can use the Expand strategy when a child provides a one-word response or an incomplete response. For example, in the *Hello Lighthouse* dialogue in Textbox 3.1 when the adult asks the child if they know what the light does in a lighthouse, the child responds, "Keeps boats from crashing." This is an incomplete sentence and does not explain the exact purpose of the light. So, the adult provides the expansion saying, "That's right. The lighthouse shines a light and shows ships where the rocks are so they don't crash into them."

The <u>E</u>xpand strategy is also useful for helping children learn new vocabulary words in the story (the <u>E</u>ncouraging vocabulary strategy). For example, in *The Patchwork Quilt* dialogue in Textbox 3.2, the adult and child are discussing what *masterpiece* means. After the adult explains the meaning of the word in a way that the child can understand, the adult asks the child to repeat what *masterpiece* means (the encourage <u>R</u>epetition strategy is explained in the next section). The child's repetition is not quite a full explanation of the word *masterpiece* ("It's like my painting, that's something very special"). To encourage a more elaborate definition, the adult uses an <u>E</u>xpansion by saying, "Yes, it's something you make that's very unique and everyone admires it."

It is okay if the child does not give a complete and elaborate description of a vocabulary word on the first try. The process of learning a word's meaning requires multiple exposures to the word and multiple opportunities for the child to actively process its meaning.[8] Children need to use these new words in context and receive appropriate feedback from adults.[9] When a word is repeated throughout a story, stopping multiple times to discuss the word in that context will allow the child to further refine their understanding of the word's meaning.

ENCOURAGE REPETITION

Once the adult provides an expansion, the next step is to ask the child to repeat the expanded language form. This is the encourage <u>R</u>epetition strategy. For example, in the *Hello Lighthouse* dialogue after the adult's expansion, saying "The lighthouse shines a light and shows ships where the rocks are," the adult then asks the child to repeat this more elaborate explanation by saying, "Now you tell me, what does the light do in the lighthouse?"

The Patchwork Quilt dialogue also provides several examples of <u>R</u>epetition. The first is when the adult explains what a patchwork quilt is from the cover of the book. Other examples are when the adult and child discuss the meaning of the words *anxious* and *masterpiece*.

Encouraging the child to repeat the adult's expanded utterance allows the child to take ownership of these new language forms.

Expanding on the child's response and encouraging Repetition are often the most challenging techniques to employ while reading with a child.[10,11] In the context of the reading session, the adult might feel awkward about asking the child to repeat something they just said. It seems unnatural or artificial because in everyday language we do not ask the conversational participant to repeat what we have just said. However, regular use of these strategies throughout storybook reading is essential to helping the child develop more advanced oral language.

As adults continue to practice the encouraging Repetition strategy and as they further develop rapport with the child, they will become more comfortable with asking the child to repeat what the adult suggested. It might also help to find creative ways to ask the child to repeat the adult's expanded language. For example, you might gently request a repetition by saying, "Now remind me . . ." This type of phrase might make it seem like the request for repetition is a more natural part of the conversation and less like you are asking for a correct response.

EVALUATE

The Evaluate strategy involves the adult providing praise and encouragement for the child's response, feedback, and sometimes even scaffolding in the form of hints, clues, or suggestions. Several examples of praise in the form of "That's right!" can be seen in the dialogues for both books shown in textboxes 3.1 and 3.2. This is a quick way to affirm the child's response and move on.

Even better examples of praise can be found in *The Patchwork Quilt* dialogue when the adult says, "That's a great way to explain anxious" and "That's a really good prediction." These are examples of specific praise, as contrasted with generic praise like "Good job." Specific praise is more effective because it provides information about what the child did well, which promotes a sense of mastery and intrinsic motivation.[12,13]

When providing feedback on a child's response that is not quite correct, the adult can acknowledge the child's attempt and gently reframe their response into a more correct version.

- For example, in the *Hello Lighthouse* dialogue when the child attempts to define *tending*, the adult responds "That's close. Tending means taking care of."
- Likewise, in *The Patchwork Quilt* dialogue the adult responds to the child's attempt to explain the meaning of *anxious* by saying, "That's close. Sometimes anxious means worried. But here Tanya is anxious to go outside." The adult continues by asking, "Do you think she *really, really* wants to go outside?" This is a good example of scaffolding, a hint at the fact that *anxious* in this context means really wanting to do something.

The term "evaluate" was used by the researchers who created the original dialogic reading approach.[14] So, it became part of the EMPOWERED acronym in the DRIVE approach. However, *evaluation* does not mean that the adult is making a judgment about the child's response, such as whether it is correct or incorrect.

In the DRIVE approach, the purpose of questioning the child frequently throughout the story is to encourage the development of children's vocabulary and oral language through a fun and interactive process. Often, children who struggle with reading initially approach DRIVE reading sessions with apprehension because they assume that the questioning is like what is typically done in schools where the teacher asks a question and is looking for a correct-answer response. Remember that Evaluate focuses on affirming what the child has said and encouraging them to move beyond their current level of understanding.

DISTANCING

The last strategy in the EMPOWERED acronym is the Distancing prompt. The term "distancing" was used by the original researchers of dialogic reading and retained in the DRIVE approach.[15] Distancing refers to making connections with the reading material that go beyond the context of the story or are "distanced" from the here and now in the story. This means asking the child questions that encourage them to think of examples in their personal life that relate to the characters or events in the story.

Adults can use a Distancing prompt right at the beginning of the reading session when discussing the title and cover picture. This strategy is illustrated in the *Hello Lighthouse* dialogue in Box 3.1 when the child says they saw a lighthouse at the beach, and the adult asks "Did you get to go inside the lighthouse?" Notice that this question goes beyond the context of the story to draw on the child's personal experiences that the adult can then bring back to the story.

Keep in mind that it is possible some children may never have seen a lighthouse. In this case, the adult might ask the child questions about whether they have gone to a beach and what they have seen. It is also possible that a child has never been to a beach. Taking the time to discuss beaches and lighthouses before reading provides the child with necessary prior knowledge for comprehending the story.

Distancing prompts also are useful for encouraging children to make connections to the characters such as what characters may be feeling or why they may have acted in a certain way. An example of this is found in the *Hello Lighthouse* dialogue in Textbox 3.1 when the adult asks the child, "Have you ever felt lonely?" When the child responds about feeling lonely at recess, this links the child's personal experience to the experience of the keeper in the story. This example also illustrates how Distancing prompts can be used to foster the learning of vocabulary in the story, such as the meaning of the word *lonely*.

Using a Distancing question for Encouraging vocabulary is also illustrated in *The Patchwork Quilt* dialogue in Textbox 3.2. The adult is discussing the word *masterpiece* which appears several times throughout the story to refer to the patchwork quilt that the grandmother is making. This is an important vocabulary word for the child to understand because it supports the child's comprehension of the story. The word *masterpiece* is difficult to explain in a way that a child might understand. So, the adult follows up the Wh-question of "What's a masterpiece?" by asking, "Have you ever made a drawing or art project at school and your teacher thought it was excellent and so very beautiful? Maybe you put it on the refrigerator for everyone to see?"

As you read the remaining dialogue in Textbox 3.2 surrounding the word *masterpiece*, notice that the adult follows up on the child's personal experience by defining masterpiece in that context. The adult then encourages Repetition from the child and provides Evaluation and Expansion. Although the EMPOWERED strategies have been presented and discussed in this chapter sequentially, during the process of reading in the DRIVE approach, these strategies are often intricately intertwined.

SUMMARY

Keep in mind that you do not need to use all nine strategies during each reading session. The strategies that a reader uses with a child will depend on several factors, including the age of the child and the complexity of the story. In chapter 6, you will learn some tips for using the EMPOWERED strategies and see what strategies are typically used in actual reading sessions with children from kindergarten through Grade 3.

NOTES

1. Jessica Blom-Hoffman, Therese M. O'Neil-Pirozzi, and Joanna Cutting. "Read Together, Talk Together: The Acceptability of Teaching Parents to Use Dialogic Reading Strategies via Videotaped Instruction." *Psychology in the Schools* 43, no. 1 (2006): 71–78.
2. Grover J. Whitehurst, Jeffrey N. Epstein, Andrea L. Angell, Adam C. Payne, Deanne A. Crone, and Janet E. Fischel. "Outcomes of an Emergent Literacy Intervention in Head Start." *Journal of Educational Psychology* 86, no. 4 (1994): 542.
3. Andrea Zevenbergen and Grover Whitehurst. "Dialogic Reading: A Shared Picture Book Intervention for Preschoolers." In *On Reading Books to Children: Parents and Teachers*, ed. Anne van Kleek, Steven Stahl and Eurydice Bauer (Mahwah, NJ: Lawrence Erlbaum Associates, 2003), 177–220.
4. Barbara A. Wasik and Annemarie H. Hindman. "Realizing the Promise of Open-Ended Questions." *The Reading Teacher* 67, no. 4 (2013): 302–311. doi: 10.1002/trtr.1218.
5. Whitehurst et al., "Outcomes of an Emergent Literacy Intervention in Head Start."
6. Penny Levickis, Sheena Reilly, Luigi Girolametto, Obioha C. Ukoumunne, and Melissa Wake. "Maternal Behaviors Promoting Language Acquisition in Slow-to-Talk Toddlers." *Journal of Developmental & Behavioral Pediatrics* 35, no. 4 (May 2014): 274–281. doi: 10.1097/DBP.0000000000000056.

7. Nancy J. Scherer, and Lesley B Olswang. "Role of Mothers' Expansions in Stimulating Children's Language Production." *Journal of Speech and Hearing Research* 27, no. September (1984): 387–96.

8. William E. Nagy, Richard C. Anderson, and Patricia A. Herman. "Learning Word Meanings From Context During Normal Reading." *American Educational Research Journal* 24, no. 2 (1987): 237–70. doi: 10.3102/00028312024002237.

9. Catherine S. Tamis-LeMonda, Yana Kuchirko, and Lulu Song. "Why Is Infant Language Learning Facilitated by Parental Responsiveness?" *Current Directions in Psychological Science* 23, no. 2 (2014): 121–26. doi: 10.1177/0963721414522813.

10. Carrie Faber. "Replicating the Treatment Fidelity of POWERED Strategies in the Dialogic Reading with Integrated Vocabulary Enrichment Intervention" (Poster presented at the annual meeting of the New England Psychological Association, Worcester, MA, November 2018).

11. Stephanie Kaesmann. "Evaluating Treatment Fidelity of EMPOWERED Strategies in a Kindergarten Dialogic Reading Intervention" (Poster presented at the annual meeting of the Northeastern Educational Research Association, online, October 2021).

12. Jennifer Henderlong Corpus, and Mark R. Lepper. "The Effects of Person versus Performance Praise on Children's Motivation: Gender and Age as Moderating Factors." *Educational Psychology* 27, no. 4 (2007): 487–508. doi: 10.1080/01443410601159852.

13. Shannon R. Zentall and Bradley J. Morris. "'Good Job, You're so Smart': The Effects of Inconsistency of Praise Type on Young Children's Motivation." *Journal of Experimental Child Psychology* 107, no. 2 (2010): 155–63. doi: 10.1016/j.jecp.2010.04.015.

14. Grover J. Whitehurst, Francine L. Falco, Christopher J. Lonigan, Janet E. Fischel, Barbara D. DeBaryshe, Marta C. Valdez-Menchaca, and Marie Caulfield. "Accelerating Language Development through Picture Book Reading." *Developmental Psychology* 24, no. 4 (1988): 552–559.

15. Andrea Zevenbergen and Grover Whitehurst. "Dialogic Reading: A Shared Picture Book Intervention for Preschoolers." In *On Reading Books to Children: Parents and Teachers*, ed. Anne van Kleek, Steven Stahl and Eurydice Bauer (Mahwah, NJ: Lawrence Erlbaum Associates, 2003), 177–220.

Chapter 4

Encouraging Vocabulary

The relationship between vocabulary, or knowing what a word means, and reading development was introduced in chapter 1. You may recall the distinction between the number of words a child knows (breadth of knowledge) and how well they know the meaning of a word (depth of knowledge). A key goal in vocabulary development is to increase the number of words that a child has access to while emphasizing a deep understanding of those words. The present chapter will further elaborate on the role of vocabulary knowledge in reading comprehension with a specific emphasis on how the DRIVE approach can be used to encourage vocabulary.

ENCOURAGING VOCABULARY IN EVERYDAY INTERACTIONS

The most important activity parents and caregivers can do with their children right from birth is talk with them. There are many types of language interactions between caregivers and young children that occur during daily activities.

- Adults label objects that children are attending to in the environment (called joint attention).
- They use verbal prompts ("Let's clean up the toys").
- They also ask questions, respond to children's questions, and respond to children's brief utterances ("Want juice") with longer, more elaborate sentences, called expansions ("Yes, I'll give you the juice").

Parents and caregivers who frequently engage in these interactions tend to have children with more developed language skills.[1,2] Also, when adults initiate conversations, answer questions, and create a dialogue with their toddlers and preschoolers, these behaviors encourage conversational turn-taking (a back-and-forth exchange between caregiver and child). This turn-taking promotes the development of vocabulary and oral language skills.[3,4]

From birth to age three, children rapidly acquire both expressive vocabulary and receptive vocabulary. Expressive vocabulary refers to words that an individual can produce when speaking or writing, whereas receptive vocabulary refers to words that a person understands when reading or listening. For example, a toddler may be able to understand the word "tired" (receptive vocabulary) but may not be able to say it to express how they feel (expressive vocabulary).

Parents and caregivers can begin to see signs of expressive and receptive vocabulary when children are about six months of age. Expressive language begins with babbling around six months and first words between eight and eighteen months of age. Receptive language also begins to emerge around six to twelve months, with infants recognizing their own names and objects or concepts that they frequently hear.[5,6]

Around eighteen months, children typically experience a "vocabulary spurt" in their expressive language where the rate of producing new words speeds up.[7,8] By about age three, children have an expressive vocabulary of 360 to 630 words and an even larger receptive vocabulary.[9,10] Vocabulary development continues from preschool age through the elementary years and into adolescence at a rate of several new words per day, with ranges of about 6,000 words for six-year-olds to about 40,000 words for the average ten-year-old.[11,12]

Having a strong vocabulary is important for becoming a good reader. Vocabulary development in early childhood supports the development of literacy skills such as knowledge of letters, words, and concepts about print, even before children start school.[13] This early knowledge of word meanings helps children more readily recognize words that they are learning to decode (using knowledge of letter-sound patterns to sound out written words).[14] It is easier to identify or sound out a word in print if you have heard it before. In sum, vocabulary knowledge leads to long-term positive outcomes such as good reading comprehension, higher reading achievement, and better school achievement overall.[15,16]

ENCOURAGING VOCABULARY THROUGH SHARED BOOK READING

Parents and caregivers can encourage the development of expressive and receptive vocabulary, not only through talking with their children, but also through shared book reading. During shared reading, children are exposed to vocabulary that they typically do not hear in their everyday activities.

Much of what children hear in everyday language is "contextualized." This means they have many sources of information to help figure out a word's meaning such as the physical surroundings, gestures, and intonation.[17] For example, imagine that a parent points to a kiwi (a word the child has never heard) and says, "Do you want to try some of my kiwi?" The word refers to a particular object, and the context of the situation together with the gesture enables the child to figure out what the word means. On the other hand, vocabulary that children encounter in stories is "decontextualized," meaning that it is abstract and removed from the here and now.[18]

Picture story books do provide exposure to concrete words and often use pictures to provide a context to support understanding of new words. However, stories also provide an opportunity to learn many new words that are not concrete and that children do not encounter in everyday life. As examples, children may:

- be exposed to adjectives such as *amazing*, *mischievous*, *mysterious*, and *perplexed*;
- learn action verbs such as *bellow*, *quiver*, *scamper*, and *scatter*; and
- encounter adverbs that describe actions such as *angrily*, *cleverly*, and *fiercely*.

During shared reading, taking the time to stop and discuss unfamiliar words such as these can promote vocabulary development in young children.[19]

ENCOURAGING VOCABULARY USING EMPOWERED STRATEGIES

Parents and caregivers can promote vocabulary development during shared reading using several of the EMPOWERED strategies in the DRIVE approach. Before discussing how to use the strategies to encourage vocabulary, it is important to know which words to select. Not all words are equally important to focus on.

Researcher Isabel Beck and colleagues describe three types of words that appear in reading material—Tier 1, Tier 2, and Tier 3 words.[20] Tier 1 words are common words encountered in everyday life, such as *apple*, *boy*, and *park*. Adults do not need to focus on the meaning of these words while reading because children likely already have these in their oral vocabulary. Adults also will not encounter Tier 3 words in story books for young children. These words are typically very specialized vocabulary found in specific academic disciplines, such as *siege*, *hypotenuse*, and *soluble*.

The words that adults should focus on are referred to as Tier 2 words. These words are not typically found in everyday language and are often used in stories to describe characters and emotions.[21] Tier 2 words are also useful for children to know because they appear across multiple contexts and sometimes their meanings can change depending on context.[22,23] For example, in *Brave Irene* by William Steig, Irene traveled through a snowstorm to deliver a handmade dress to the duchess, and the duchess was delirious to see her. In this context, *delirious* means very excited and overjoyed. In another story, *delirious* may mean that someone is confused and not able to think or speak clearly usually because they are sick.

When reading with children, look for Tier 2 words to select and discuss. A general rule of thumb is to choose words that (1) are interesting and useful for children to know, (2) will help with the overall comprehension of the story, and (3) you can define or explain in a way that children will understand.[24] Table 4.1 provides sample books that contain suggested words for encouraging vocabulary when reading using the DRIVE approach. Preview the book before reading to select one or two words per page that you might discuss, but it is fine if there are no appropriate words on a page or several pages.

As discussed earlier, the aim is not for the child to learn a dictionary definition of the word. Instead, the goal is to encourage the child to actively process the meaning of the word in a way that they can take ownership of the word and incorporate it into their vocabulary.[25] Children need to use the words in context to convey their ideas and get feedback from adults.[26] The best way to do this is to ask the child questions and engage them in a discussion about certain vocabulary words instead of just rephrasing the meaning of the words.

Encouraging Vocabulary 45

Table 4.1 Sample Books for Encouraging Vocabulary Using the DRIVE Approach

Title	Author	Vocabulary Words
Hello Lighthouse	Sophie Blackall	disappear, gathering, guiding, disaster, journey, reply, tending, unexpected
Flat Stanley: His Original Adventure	Jeff Brown	altered, angrily, brave, carefully, cleverly, discovered, enormous, frightened, gloomy, gracefully, hardy, hurried/hurrying, jealous, pretended, realized, recognize, terrifying
The Little House	Virginia Lee Burton	curious, elevated, gathered, glance, frightened, hurried, lonely, wondered
The Enormous Crocodile	Roald Dahl	bravest, clever, enormous, gigantic, greedy, shriek
The Patchwork Quilt	Valerie Flournoy	anxious, carefully, delicately, examined, gazed, lonely, mischievous, miserable, plead, realized, restlessly, scattered, sparkling
Earthquack!	Margie Palatini	calmly, cleverly, convinced, commotion, crumbling, disguised, interrupting, sneaky, tumble
The Bravest Dog Ever: The True Story of Balto	Natalie Standiford	brave/bravery/bravest, calm, famous, hero, hitched, panic, proudly, terrible
Brave Irene	William Steig	brave, ceased, cherished, clasped, clutching, delirious, disappear, gazing/gazed, hurried, ordinary, pounced, radiant, shrieked, wondered
Doctor De Soto	William Steig	bravely, delicate, dangerous, exclaimed, misery, promptly, serious, stunned, wailed, wicked, wondered, worrying, unique
Sylvester and the Magic Pebble	William Steig	amaze, disappeared, dreadful, frantic, frightened, helpless, hopeless, inquiring, miserable, mysterious, paced, puzzled, remarkable, startled, unusual, vanished, wondering
What Do You with an Idea?	Kobi Yamada	amazing, attention, idea, discovered, fragile, opportunity, strange, wondered
What Do You with a Problem?	Kobi Yamada	disappear, disguise, ignoring, problem, realized, worry/worried

To engage in a discussion of vocabulary words, adults can use the EMPOWERED strategies of asking Wh-questions or Open-ended questions. For example, "What does *lonely* mean?" Adults can explain what the word means if the child does not know at all. However, first try other approaches that will provide scaffolding to help the child acquire the meaning of the word. Use the strategy, Make it fun, by incorporating gestures and mime to scaffold the meaning. For the word *giggle*, you can demonstrate giggling and then have the child do it. Or, for the word *amaze*, ask the child to show you the facial expression of a person who is amazed at something.

Adults can also use a Distancing prompt, which is a way to connect the vocabulary word to the child's personal experience. To introduce the meaning of the word *patient*, the adult can ask the child, "When have you been patient?" If the child does not respond, the adult can use scaffolding and provide their own example first. The adult might say, "I was patient when I had to wait in a long line at the store. Would you be patient if you had to wait for a long time?" Connecting the word to an activity or experience the child may have outside of the story is an example of "decontextualized" vocabulary, as discussed earlier.

Do not be satisfied with the child's mime, gesture, or initial response to a Distancing question (e.g., "Yes, I would be patient."). After this interaction, be sure to ask the child to state what the word means. For example, an adult might ask, "So, now, what does patient mean?" If the child still does not verbalize a response, the adult can provide a definition.

Alternatively, if the child gives a brief or incomplete response ("patient means waiting"), the adult can model a more appropriate explanation of the word. For example, the adult might say, "Patient means that you can wait a long time for something without getting angry or upset." This is an example of the Expansion strategy in which the adult takes a brief response the child gave and expands on it to provide a more sophisticated sentence.

Once the adult provides the modeled language, it is also important to use the encourage Repetition strategy. For example, after modeling the more sophisticated definition, the adult might say, "Now, remind me what patient means." As previously mentioned in chapters 2 and 3, research suggests that this strategy is challenging for adults to use.[27] It feels awkward to ask the child to once again provide a definition.

However, encouraging the child to repeat the expanded sentence modeled by the adult will help the child take ownership of the word.

GENERAL GUIDELINES TO CONSIDER

While planning ahead and knowing what words to focus on is important, remember that explaining vocabulary is done within the dialogue of the story. With the exception of asking a question about a vocabulary word that is in the title of the book, there is no need to pre-teach the meaning of the words before reading the story. Planning ahead simply means that you know what words you will focus on. Explaining the words and focusing on meaning should happen as the words occur and within the context of the story. This will help children to use what they already know and what has already happened in the story to begin to understand these unfamiliar words.

Choosing Words to Focus On

Some words may be unfamiliar to children even though they are not necessarily Tier 2 words. Do not spend time creating a dialogue around these words if they are not central to the story. Instead, provide a brief explanation at the point in the story when the word appears, as needed.[28]

For example, in *The Bravest Dog Ever: The True Story of Balto* by Natalie Standiford (shown in table 4.1), the author discusses Balto's work as a sled dog, carrying food and tools to *miners*. Children may not know what a miner is, but the word is not central to the story. So, a quick explanation before moving on is all that is needed. On the other hand, the meaning of words like *brave*, *bravery*, and *bravest* is important to discuss in order to comprehend the story of Balto's heroic efforts.

Another example comes from the book *Carmela Full of Wishes* by Matt De La Pena. In this story as Carmela is riding her scooter past some fields, she smells *manure*. Many children may not know what this word means, and similar to the word *miner* above in the story about Balto, it is not central to the story. But stopping to explain will help children understand what is happening in the accompanying picture. And it may also be an opportunity to use the Make it fun strategy to discuss a word that many children will find funny!

Number of Words

While you do not want to spend time discussing words that are not central to the story, you also do not want to take too much time discussing multiple vocabulary words on a single page. This is excessive, and many children will be frustrated or bored with the questioning. A good rule of thumb is to focus on no more than three words on a page. But this is not a hard and fast rule; the number of words will depend on the amount of text on the page and the number of Tier 2 or relevant words. Compare these two examples from table 4.1.

- In *The Little House* by Virginia Lee Burton, one page contains very little text but two important words, *curious* and *wondered*. The next page has no vocabulary words. So, it would be fine to stop and discuss both of these words.
- *The Enormous Crocodile* by Roald Dahl has a great deal more text on each page. On a single page, there are several vocabulary words that are important: *greedy*, *bravest*, *clever*, and *enormous*. The word *enormous* appears on the previous page and is repeated throughout the story. The word *clever* appears here for the first time and is repeated throughout the book. So, it would be a good idea to discuss *clever* here in addition to *greedy* and *bravest* and skip *enormous* on this page.

Reminders When Words Are Repeated

When reading with a child using the same book over multiple sessions, draw attention to a vocabulary word that is repeated throughout the book. Use a <u>Wh</u>-question, such as "We've seen this word before. What does this word mean?" Another way to re-introduce a recurring vocabulary word might be: "Hmm. Does that word sound familiar? What does ____ mean?" Alternatively, you might state in a playful voice, "There's that word again! What does ____ mean?"

As an example, in *The Enormous Crocodile* by Roald Dahl (shown in table 4.1), the crocodile uses the word *clever* to refer to the tricks he is planning for trying to catch a child to eat. He repeats the phrase "clever tricks" throughout the story. Do not assume that children will remember the meaning of the word from a dialogue you had earlier in the story, especially if it was on a previous day.

- The phrase *clever* trick is first introduced on the second page of the book when the Enormous Crocodile says, "Nobody will see me," he said, "because this time I've thought up secret plans and clever tricks." This phrase is repeated several times on the following pages and can be reinforced as you go along.
- One really good place to reinforce the meaning would be when the crocodile tries his first clever trick with his plan to pretend to be a coconut tree to catch the children. When the plan fails (with a wonderful picture of the hippopotamus knocking down the "coconut tree"), you could ask the Open-ended question: "Now, was that a 'clever' trick?" This will give children an opportunity to explain how this wasn't very clever!

As discussed in chapter 3, children need multiple exposures to a word in which they actively process its meaning in order to create a long-term representation of the word's meaning.[29] The more often a word is emphasized within a session or across different books, the more likely the child will begin to remember the meaning of the word.

Highlight Words from Previous Books

When reading with the same child using different books, highlight words that have been in previous stories by using a Wh-question, such as "When have we seen this word before?" For example, the word *brave* appears in multiple books shown in table 4.1, such as *Brave Irene* and *Doctor De Soto* by William Steig, *The Bravest Dog Ever: The True Story of Balto* by Natalie Standiford, and *The Enormous Crocodile* by Roald Dahl. Children learn the meanings of words gradually by encountering them many times and using them in different contexts.[30,31]

Use of Pictures

Use pictures sparingly. It is acceptable to stop at a picture as a way to discuss what is happening in the story at that point, especially when reading with toddlers and preschoolers. However, it is not recommended to use pictures as clues to try to identify a word or guess at its meaning. This will be discussed in greater detail in chapter 6.

For now, here is an example of using a picture appropriately. In *The Bravest Dog Ever: The True Story of Balto* by Natalie Standiford, readers encounter the word *hitched* at several points in the story, as when the driver hitched the dogs to the sled. This word is important for understanding the story, especially since some children might not be familiar with sled dogs. So, the adult can use the picture of the sled and reins to explain what hitched means.

SUMMARY

Oral vocabulary is crucial for becoming a good reader. Parents and caregivers can encourage the development of vocabulary through many everyday interactions including shared book reading. While reading to children using the DRIVE approach, adults can apply many of the EMPOWERED strategies to encourage vocabulary development. Remember to select words for dialogue that are interesting and useful for children to know, central to understanding the story, and easy for you to explain in a way that children will understand. Encouraging vocabulary in this way can contribute to an increase in the sheer number of words that a child knows as well as deepen their understanding of those words.

NOTES

1. Catherine Snow, Patton Tabors, and David Dickinson. "Language Development in the Preshool Years, ed. David Dickinson and Patton Tabors." In *Beginning Literacy With Language* (Baltimore, MD: Brookes, 2001).

2. Catherine S. Tamis-LeMonda, Marc H. Bornstein, and Lisa Baumwell. "Maternal Responsiveness and Children's Achievement of Language Milestones." *Child Development* 72, no. 3 (2001): 748–67. doi: 10.1111/1467-8624.00313.

3. Jill Gilkerson, Jeffrey A. Richards, Steven F. Warren, D. Kimbrough Oller, Rosemary Russo, and Betty Vohr. "Language Experience in the Second Year of Life and Language Outcomes in Late Childhood." *Pediatrics* 142, no. 4 (2018): e20174276. doi: 10.1542/peds.2017-4276.

4. Rachel R. Romeo, Julia A. Leonard, Sydney T. Robinson, Martin R. West, Allyson P. Mackey, Meredith L. Rowe, and John D.E. Gabrieli. "Beyond the 30-Million-Word Gap: Children's Conversational Exposure Is Associated With Language-Related Brain Function." *Psychological Science* 29, no. 5 (2018): 700–710. doi: 10.1177/0956797617742725.

5. Heather Bortfeld, James L. Morgan, Roberta Michnick Golinkoff, and Karen Rathbun. "Mommy and Me." *Psychological Science* 16, no. 4 (2005): 298–304. doi: 10.1111/j.0956-7976.2005.01531.x.

6. Caroline Phythian-Sence and Richard Wagner. "Vocabulary Acquisition: A Primer." In *Vocabulary Acquisition: Implications for Reading Comprehension*, 1–14 (New York: Guliford Press, 2007).

7. Lois Bloom. *One Word At a Time: The Use of Single Word Utterances Before Syntax* (The Hague, The Netherlands: Mouton, 1973).

8. Bob McMurray. "Defusing the Childhood Vocabulary Explosion." *Science* 317, no. 5838 (2007): 631. doi: 10.1126/science.1144073.

9. Larry Fenson, Philip S. Dale, J. Steven Reznick, Elizabeth Bates, Donna J. Thal, and J. Pethick Stephen. "Variability in Communicative Development." *Monographs of the Society for Research in Child Development* 59, no. 242 (1994).

10. Michael Tomasello. *Constructing A Language: A Usage-Based Theory of Language Acquisition* (Cambridge, MA: Harvard University Press, 2003).

11. Jeremy M. Anglin, George A. Miller, and Pamela C. Wakefield. "Vocabulary Development: A Morphological Analysis." *Monographs of the Society for Research in Child Development* 58, no. 10 (1993): i. doi: 10.2307/1166112.

12. C. J. Johnson and J. M. Anglin. "Qualitative Developments in the Content and Form of Children's Definitions." *Journal of Speech and Hearing Research* 38, no. 3 (1995): 612–29. doi: 10.1044/jshr.3803.612.

13. Sebastian Suggate, Elizabeth Schaughency, Helena McAnally, and Elaine Reese. "From Infancy to Adolescence: The Longitudinal Links between Vocabulary, Early Literacy Skills, Oral Narrative, and Reading Comprehension." *Cognitive Development* 47, no. April (2018): 82–95. doi: 10.1016/j.cogdev.2018.04.005.

14. National Early Literacy Panel. 2008. *Developing Early Literacy: Report of the National Early Literacy Panel* (Washington, DC: National Institute for Literacy).

15. Ludo Verhoeven, Jan van Leeuwe, and Anne Vermeer. "Vocabulary Growth and Reading Development across the Elementary School Years." *Scientific Studies of Reading* 15, no. 1 (2011): 8–25.

16. Suggate et al., "From Infancy to Adolescence: The Longitudinal Links between Vocabulary, Early Literacy Skills, Oral Narrative, and Reading Comprehension."

17. Margaret G. McKeown. "Effective Vocabulary Instruction Fosters Knowing Words, Using Words, and Understanding How Words Work." *Language, Speech, and Hearing Services in Schools* 50, no. 4 (2019): 466–76. doi: 10.1044/2019_LSHSS-VOIA-18-0126.

18. Meredith L. Rowe. "Decontextualized Language Input and Preschoolers' Vocabulary Development." *Seminars in Speech and Language* 34, no. 4 (2013): 260–66. doi: 10.1055/s-0033-1353444.

19. Barbara A. Wasik, Annemarie H. Hindman, and Emily K. Snell. "Book Reading and Vocabulary Development: A Systematic Review." *Early Childhood Research Quarterly* 37 (2016): 39–57. doi: 10.1016/j.ecresq.2016.04.003.

20. Isabel Beck, Margaret McKeown, and Linda Kucan. *Bringing Words to Life: Robust Vocabulary Instruction* (New York: Guilford Press, 2002).

21. McKeown. "Effective Vocabulary Instruction Fosters Knowing Words, Using Words, and Understanding How Words Work."

22. Ibid.

23. Beck et al., *Bringing Words to Life: Robust Vocabulary Instruction*, 2nd ed.

24. Ibid.

25. Wasik et al., "Book Reading and Vocabulary Development: A Systematic Review."

26. Catherine S. Tamis-LeMonda, Yana Kuchirko, and Lulu Song. "Why Is Infant Language Learning Facilitated by Parental Responsiveness?" *Current Directions in Psychological Science* 23, no. 2 (2014): 121–26. doi: 10.1177/0963721414522813.

27. Brianna Chiaraluce. "Evaluating the Treatment Fidelity of a Dialogic Reading Intervention" (Poster presented at the annual meeting of the Northeastern Educational Research Association, Trumbull, CT, October 2018).

28. Margaret McKeown and Isabel Beck. "Taking Advantage of Read-Alouds to Help Children." In *On Reading Books to Children: Parents and Teachers*, ed. Anne van Kleek, Steven Stahl, and Eurydice Bauer, 159–176 (Mahwah, NJ: Lawrence Erlbaum Associates, 2003).

29. William E. Nagy, Richard C. Anderson, and Patricia A. Herman. "Learning Word Meanings From Context During Normal Reading." *American Educational Research Journal* 24, no. 2 (1987): 237–70. doi: 10.3102/00028312024002237.

30. Richard Anderson and William Nagy. "Word Meanings." In *Handbook Of Reading Research, Vol. 2*, ed. Rebecca Barr, Michael Kamil, Peter Mosenthal, and P. David Pearson (Mahwah, NJ: Lawrence Erlbaum, 1991), 690–724.

31. Susan Goldin-Meadow, Susan C. Levine, Larry V. Hedges, Janellen Huttenlocher, Stephen W. Raudenbush, and Steven L. Small. "New Evidence about Language and Cognitive Development Based on a Longitudinal Study: Hypotheses for Intervention." *American Psychologist* 69, no. 6 (2014): 588–599.

Chapter 5

Choosing a Book

Before beginning a reading session, it is important to select an appropriate book and plan the reading session. DRIVE works best when the reader has read the book ahead of time and generally mapped out where to ask questions. Other questions may occur naturally as you discuss the book with an individual child or group of children, and sometimes children themselves will ask questions, but planning ahead allows the reader to make the most out of a DRIVE session.

While keeping a few key points in mind, there is no "wrong" book. As a general rule of thumb, choose books that have an interesting story structure and rich vocabulary, that encourage open-ended questions, and that are worth discussing in depth.

The original researchers recommended that the best books for dialogic reading have clear illustrations, relatively little text, and an engaging story.[1] However, this is because their approach was focused more on younger preschool-age children. In DRIVE, the most appropriate books will also have an engaging story but books that are appropriate for DRIVE should have enough text in order to allow for adequate questioning about the story while also emphasizing vocabulary.

What makes a book engaging or interesting? This is going to depend on a number of different factors such as the individual interests of both the child and reader and the age or developmental level of the child/ children. While the story needs to be engaging, an interesting story structure does not mean that the book needs to be lengthy or necessarily have a lot of text per page. For example, *Hello Lighthouse* by Sophie

Blackall (discussed in chapter 3) is relatively short, but the nature of the topic, the vocabulary used, and the story can generate many questions and lead to a rich conversation with the child or children being read to.

A book that has a storyline that coincides with a particular time of year, holiday, or topic being discussed at school can also generate interest and allow for lots of <u>W</u>h-questions and <u>D</u>istancing prompts. For example, *Wild Child* by Lynn Plourde is a perfect choice to discuss the changes that come in the fall. Other books by Lynn Plourde focus on summer (*Summer's Vacation*), spring (*Spring's Sprung*) and winter (*Winter Waits*). Having a few books in mind, knowing the general interests of the child/children you will be reading with, and planning ahead will help you to decide whether a book is engaging.

TYPES OF BOOKS

In school, teachers often provide books to children for independent reading practice that are supposed to be "just right" for them to read on their own. This is called a child's "independent reading level." During an independent reading at school, children typically read "easy readers" (also referred to as decodable books or leveled books) which are often fairly simple stories written using text that is easily decodable. Specifically, the words used in these books follow phonics patterns that the developing reader is familiar with. While these books are very important for reading instruction and practice, they are often limited in story structure and vocabulary.

As the child is not the one reading in most cases, the book chosen for DRIVE does not need to be at the specific reading level of the child. Again, books used in the DRIVE approach should encourage conversation and expose the child to new vocabulary. Most easy readers generally don't contain enough text to be an appropriate choice.

Many of the recommended books throughout the previous chapters, such as *Sylvester and the Magic Pebble* or *The Patchwork Quilt*, are what are often referred to as picture books. Picture books use both words and illustrations to tell a story. Some other well-known examples include *Blueberries for Sal* by Robert McCloskey and *Trombone Shorty* by Troy Andrews. These picture story books are an excellent choice for early readers, usually children in kindergarten through second grade, although depending on the complexity of the story, older children may benefit as well.

While the illustrations in picture books often coincide with and add to the meaning of the text, these illustrations don't always accurately predict the story. Remember that the goal of DRIVE is to engage the child in a conversation about the story, and while using pictures that accompany the words may be a good starting point, the focus should really be the text itself. Chapter 6 will discuss in more detail how to appropriately use pictures while reading using the DRIVE approach.

Although picture books are often recommended for younger children, a book does not need to have pictures to use DRIVE. Many early chapter books such as *Flat Stanley* by Jeff Brown, *Junie B Jones* by Barbara Park, or *A to Z Mysteries* by Ron Roy are great choices for slightly older children (typically grades 1–4). These types of books are sometimes referred to as "bridge books" as they are a bridge between the early, easy readers mentioned above, and lengthier, more challenging chapter books.

WHO IS READING AND WHEN?

Book choice might also depend on who is doing the reading and when. A librarian at story hour may need to find a shorter book that can be completed in one session and that appeals to a group of children. Similarly, a caregiver might want a shorter book if reading before bedtime. A couple of great examples include *What Do You Do with an Idea?* by Kobi Yamada or *Bear Came Along* by Richard Morris.

Note that shorter books are not necessarily just for younger children. Books like *What Do You Do with an Idea?* (and *What Do You Do with a Problem?* also by Kobi Yamada) will appeal to a wide age range and the dialogue can be adapted to the developmental level of the child. For example, in *What Do You Do with an Idea?* the character is worried that his idea is silly. And when he shares it, he is made fun of. While older children may have experience with being ridiculed for something they have done, younger children may have a harder time understanding that this character is being made fun of for what he thinks. Because the concept of an idea is somewhat abstract, you may need to spend more

Table 5.1 Picture Books that Can Be Read in One Sitting

Title	Author	Grade Level
Hello Lighthouse	Sophie Blackall	Prek–3
The Hat	Jan Brett	Prek–K
Carmela Full of Wishes	Matt De La Pena	Prek–3
How Many Stars in the Sky?	Lenny Hort	K–1
The Wolf's Chicken Stew	Keiko Kasza	K–1
A Most Unusual Day	Sydra Mallery	Prek–3
Bear Came Along	Richard Morris	Prek–3
Wild Child (and others in series by the same author)	Lynn Plourde	Prek–2
The Relatives Came	Cynthia Rylant	Prek–2
What Do You Do with an Idea? and What Do You Do with a Problem?	Kobi Yamada	K–3

time discussing this vocabulary word with younger children who tend to be more focused on the concrete.

Additionally, a shorter book that is a bit more open-ended like *What Do You Do with an Idea?* might be especially good for a child who is initially hesitant to engage in a dialogue. A shorter book may not seem as overwhelming as a longer story with a lot of text. Also, the questions can be framed so that it feels more like a casual conversation. This may help a reluctant or shy child to feel a little more comfortable engaging in a dialogue. Table 5.1 provides some additional suggestions for shorter books.

However, if you will be reading with the same child or a small group over multiple sessions, you can choose a book that is lengthier. Some lengthier picture books for younger children include some of the books that have been mentioned previously such as *The Patchwork Quilt* and *Sylvester and the Magic Pebble*. Additionally, chapter books are great for slightly older children when reading can be done over multiple sessions. Some chapter books that work well for implementing DRIVE include *The Magic Tree House* series by Mary Pope Osborne (grades 3–7) or the *Mercy Watson* series by Kate DiCamillo (grades 1–4).

Other examples of lengthier picture books and chapter books are listed in tables 5.2 and 5.3. Keep in mind that when reading longer books across multiple sessions, planning in advance to target vocabulary as well as having a general idea of the story to implement EMPOWERED strategies will be important. Additionally, with a longer chapter book you might need to prepare chapter by chapter so that

Table 5.2 Picture Books to Read across Multiple Sessions

Title	Author	Grade Level
Trombone Shorty	Troy Andrews	Prek–3
Louise, the Adventures of a Chicken	Kate DiCamillo	K–3
Island Born	Junot Diaz	K–3
The Patchwork Quilt	Valerie Flournoy	Prek–3
Wilma Unlimited: How Wilma Rudolph Became the World's Fastest Woman	Kathleen Krull	K–3
The Giant Jam Sandwich	John Vernon Lord	Prek–3
Blueberries for Sal	Robert McCloskey	Prek–K
Earthquack!	Margie Palatini	Prek–3
Sylvester and the Magic Pebble	William Steig	Prek–1
Brave Irene	William Steig	K–1

you are familiar with the story. It is also important to begin a session by using <u>W</u>h-questions to help with recall of the story so far. You can also use <u>W</u>h-questions and <u>O</u>pen-ended strategies to refresh important, critical vocabulary words that you have encountered.

VOCABULARY

With DRIVE's emphasis on vocabulary (the <u>E</u>ncourage vocabulary technique in the EMPOWERED acronym), you will need books that have vocabulary words to focus on (discussed in chapter 4). As

Table 5.3 Chapter Books to Read across Multiple Sessions

Title	Author	Grade Level
Flat Stanley series	Jeff Brown	1–5
Zoey and Sassafras series	Asia Citro	K–5
Mercy Watson series	Kate DiCamillo	K–3
Nancy Clancy Super Sleuth series	Jane O'Connor	1–5
The Magic Treehouse series	Mary Pope Osborne	1–4
Junie B. Jones series	Barbara Park	1–4
The A to Z Mysteries series	Ron Roy	1–4
The Cricket in Times Square	George Selden	3–4
The Bravest Dog Ever: The True Story of Balto	Natalie Standiford	K–3
Nate the Great series	Marjorie Weinman Sharmat	1–4

mentioned before, books that are easy for readers likely will not have enough words to choose from. And even a book that has an interesting story, where there is an opportunity to discuss and use many of the EMPOWERED strategies, may not have enough (or any) vocabulary words to focus on. Again, this is where planning ahead is crucial.

So, how many vocabulary words should a book have? Research studies on shared book reading have reported a wide range in the number of vocabulary words that are focused on while reading, from two to three to over thirty-five words, with an average of about two to ten words discussed within a single reading session.[2] A good rule of thumb would be about five to ten words within a book depending on the length of the book and the amount of time spent reading. Remember you do not need to spend time on every possible vocabulary word within a given book. It is better to focus on a select few in the interest of keeping children engaged with the story.

FICTION OR NONFICTION

Most of the book recommendations in this chapter are works of fiction. However, it is possible to use nonfiction or fictionalized accounts of true stories. For example, *The Bravest Dog Ever: The True Story of Balto* by Natalie Standiford about a sled dog who brings a life-saving vaccine to an isolated town in Alaska is an engaging story that includes a good sampling of Tier 2 vocabulary words (e.g., bravest, terrible). Another example is *Wilma Unlimited: How Wilma Rudolph Became the World's Fastest Woman* by Kathleen Krull, the true story of Olympic runner Wilma Rudolph which includes themes of perseverance and overcoming adversity and also has many vocabulary words to focus on (e.g., impatience, worried).

If choosing purely nonfiction books, it will be important to make sure that the topic is interesting to the child or children being read to. In addition, the choice of vocabulary words to emphasize if using a nonfiction book needs to be carefully planned in advance as not all of the words will necessarily be important to focus on.

Nonfiction books are likely to have many Tier 3 words, which are very specialized vocabulary words found in specific settings or disciplines, as discussed in chapter 4. While it is appropriate to explain Tier 3 words to a child in order to help them grasp the meaning of what is being read, the focus should be on encouraging vocabulary through Tier 2 words (rich vocabulary words that are not found in everyday language but that can be used in multiple contexts). As discussed in chapter 4, when you come across words that are not central to the plot, including Tier 3 words, instead of spending time engaging in dialogue around these words, just give a quick explanation and move on.

BOOK FORMAT

It is recommended that you choose physical books whenever possible. It is possible to engage in meaningful shared reading using an electronic book; however, there is research to suggest that shared reading using e-books might not be optimal for encouraging comprehension and vocabulary. Some studies indicate that children are more attentive to and engaged in reading electronic books in part due to the fact that these digital platforms include animations and auditory effects that can encourage engagement.[3] Additionally, in some instances, vocabulary learning may be enhanced with electronic books that include a dictionary for unfamiliar words.[4]

However, aspects of electronic books can in fact distract a child from the story.[5,6] Many digital books contain interactive features like games and puzzles that are unrelated to understanding the story.

- When these interactive features are accessed during oral narration they can disrupt comprehension and draw children's attention away from the content of the story.[7]
- There is also evidence that when children have a choice between listening to the story being read and playing with these interactive features, they spend less time listening to the reader.[8]
- Finally, research evidence has also shown that conversations during digital book reading often focus on talking about the device or its features rather than the story itself.[9]

If you choose to use an electronic book format, here are some key points to remember. Sometimes digital books contain questions as prompts to remind adults to ask the child questions during the story. Research shows that this feature typically does not improve the child's comprehension of the story.[10] It is better to create your own questions using the

EMPOWERED strategies of <u>O</u>pen-ended questions, <u>Wh</u>-questions, and <u>D</u>istancing questions. Also, adult-initiated discussions of vocabulary words in stories yield greater benefit for encouraging vocabulary development than interactive dictionaries or static dictionaries within electronic platforms.[11]

As always, when choosing a book, you want to consider factors such as the age and developmental level of the child, as well as the child's attentiveness, interests, and preferences. For a child who is easily distracted, a print book is likely a better choice. Additionally, when reading to a group of children it is usually easier to share a physical book.

GIVE CHILDREN OPTIONS

Keeping in mind the appropriateness of the book to the child's developmental level, allow some choice in selecting books. Encouraging children to make their own choices can stimulate intrinsic motivation, a tendency to engage in an activity for its own sake or out of interest.[12,13] Choice also allows children to pick books that have stories that are interesting to them. If a child has a connection to a book or knows something about the topic, this will likely lead to more dialogue. With choice, it is usually best to offer two or at most three options for the child to pick from.

MAKE IT FUN

The choice of book can also contribute to the EMPOWERED strategy <u>M</u>ake it fun. The books you choose do not need to be serious or have a message in order to be appropriate for DRIVE. A book can be silly, play with words, contain elements of fantasy, and just generally appeal to a child or children and be a perfect choice for DRIVE.

For example, the Miss Nelson series (*Miss Nelson Is Missing*, *Miss Nelson Is Back*) by Harry Allard and James Marshall are humorous and suspenseful stories with comical illustrations that appeal to many school-age children. Additionally, these books contain lots of good Tier 2 vocabulary words (such as *misbehaved* and *refuse* in *Miss Nelson Is Missing* or *nervous* and *relieved* in *Miss Nelson Is Back*) and many

Table 5.4 Books to Encourage Make It Fun

Title	Author	Grade Level
Miss Nelson Is Missing	Harry Allard and James Marshall	K–1
Miss Nelson Is Back	Harry Allard and James Marshall	K–1
The Knight Who Was Afraid of the Dark	Barbara Shook Hazen	Prek–2
Wild Child (and others in series by the same author)	Lynn Plourde	Prek–2
Earthquack!	Margie Palatini	Prek–3
Grandpa's Teeth	Rod Clement	1–2
The Principal's New Clothes	Stephanie Calmenson	Prek–3
We Don't Eat Our Classmates	Ryan T. Higgins	K–1
The Donkey Egg	Janet Stevens and Susan Stevens Crummel	K–3
Jack and the Beanstalk and the French Fries	Mark Teague	K–2

opportunities to engage in dialogue while remaining fun. Table 5.4 has other suggestions for engaging, fun books.

For younger, preschool and kindergarten-aged children, *Wild Child* by Lynn Plourde is a great example of a book that promotes the EMPOWERED strategy Make it fun. Even though the book has a simple story structure and does not contain a lot of text, it has plenty of Tier 2 words such as *embrace* and *scatter*. Additionally, this book plays with words and rhyming, as in "Flap, flitter, birds twitter. Skitter, scatter, acorns splatter." Children find the playfulness of the words appealing and this also can promote and enhance phonological awareness, a key foundational skill for becoming a good reader, as discussed in chapter 1.

SUMMARY

Keeping the above points in mind will help you to select a book to implement DRIVE. The best book choice involves planning ahead and will depend on the reader and the child or children being read to. The examples provided in this chapter (and in other chapters in this book) will provide you with a good place to start and also help you to evaluate other books that you might use with DRIVE.

NOTES

1. Andrea Zevenbergen and Grover Whitehurst. "Dialogic Reading: A Shared Picture Book Intervention for Preschoolers." In *On Reading Books to Children: Parents and Teachers*, ed. Anne van Kleek, Steven Stahl and Eurydice Bauer (Mahwah, NJ: Lawrence Erlbaum Associates, 2003), 177–220.
2. Barbara A. Wasik, Annemarie H. Hindman, and Emily K. Snell. "Book Reading and Vocabulary Development: A Systematic Review." *Early Childhood Research Quarterly* 37 (2016): 39–57. doi: 10.1016/j.ecresq.2016.04.003.
3. Anna Richter and Mary L. Courage. "Comparing Electronic and Paper Storybooks for Preschoolers: Attention, Engagement, and Recall." *Journal of Applied Developmental Psychology* 48 (2017): 92–102.
4. May Irene Furenes, Natalia Kucirkova, and Adriana G. Bus. "A Comparison of Children's Reading on Paper Versus Screen: A Meta-Analysis." *Review of Educational Research* 91, no. 4 (2021): 483–517. doi: 10.3102/0034654321998074.
5. Tiffany G. Munzer, Alison L. Miller, Heidi M. Weeks, Niko Kaciroti, and Jenny Radesky. "Differences in Parent-Toddler Interactions with Electronic versus Print Books." *Pediatrics* 143, no. 4 (April 1, 2019). doi: 10.1542/peds.2018-2012.
6. Julia Parish-Morris, Neha Mahajan, Kathy Hirsh-Pasek, Roberta Michnick Golinkoff, and Molly Fuller Collins. "Once upon a Time: Parent-Child Dialogue and Storybook Reading in the Electronic Era." *Mind, Brain, and Education* 7, no. 3 (2013): 200–211. doi: 10.1111/mbe.12028.
7. Zsofia K. Takacs, Elise K. Swart, and Adriana G. Bus. "Benefits and Pitfalls of Multimedia and Interactive Features in Technology-Enhanced Storybooks: A Meta-Analysis." *Review of Educational Research* 85, no. 4 (2015): 698–739. doi: 10.3102/0034654314566989.
8. Maria T. de Jong and Adriana G. Bus. "Quality of Book-Reading Matters for Emergent Readers: An Experiment with the Same Book in a Regular or Electronic Format." *Journal of Educational Psychology* 94, no. 1 (2002): 145–155.
9. Furenes, et al., "A Comparison of Children's Reading on Paper Versus Screen: A Meta-Analysis."
10. Susan Rvachew, Kathrin Rees, Elizabeth Carolan, and Aparna Nadig. "Improving Emergent Literacy with School-based Shared Reading: Paper Versus ebooks." *International Journal of Child-Computer Interaction* 12 (2017): 24–29.
11. Ofra Korat, Adina Shamir, and Shani Heibal. "Expanding the Boundaries of Shared Book Reading: E-Books and Printed Books in Parent-Child

Reading as Support for Children's Language." *First Language* 33, no. 5 (2013): 504–23. doi: 10.1177/0142723713503148.

12. Erika A. Patall, Harris Cooper, and Susan R. Wynn. "The Effectiveness and Relative Importance of Choice in the Classroom." *Journal of Educational Psychology* 102, no. 4 (November 2010): 896–915. doi: 10.1037/a0019545.

13. Johnmarshall Reeve, and Hyungshim Jang. "What Teachers Say and Do to Support Students' Autonomy during a Learning Activity." *Journal of Educational Psychology* 98, no. 1 (2006): 209–18. doi: 10.1037/0022-0663.98.1.209.

Chapter 6

Tips to Consider while Reading

Now that you have learned about the general DRIVE approach and the specific EMPOWERED strategies to use while reading with children, you may have additional questions about other aspects of the reading process. This chapter provides you with advice for using the DRIVE approach while reading with children individually and in small groups.

WHO READS?

Because the original dialogic reading technique was developed for use with preschool-age children, the recommendation was for adults to read aloud to children. However, with children in the primary grades of elementary school, the adult may:

- read to the child;
- listen to the child read (with support when the child needs help); or
- take turns reading.

Some children are hesitant to read aloud at first, but as they become more comfortable with the adult, many are willing to read aloud. For struggling readers in first grade, it is recommended that you read to them, whereas in second grade, some children may want to read or take turns reading. Take your cues from the child.

HOW LONG TO READ?

There is no need to finish a book in one sitting. In fact, a good recommendation is to read with children for about ten to fifteen minutes per session over several days depending on the length and complexity of the story. It is better to take a leisurely approach to reading and using the EMPOWERED strategies than to rush to finish the story. This allows children enough time to digest the story, learn vocabulary, and experience the pleasure of reading for fun.

Taking multiple sessions to finish a story also enables the adult to start a new reading session with a recall question that is also a Wh-question, such as "What happened in the story up to this point?" If the child cannot answer, go back to earlier parts of the story and re-read or review. Reading a story over several days will convey that reading is not a chore to hastily complete, but a journey that children should savor.

USE OF EMPOWERED STRATEGIES

Chapter 3 presented a description of the EMPOWERED strategies and how they can be used during DRIVE reading sessions. It is important to realize that you do not need to use all nine strategies during each reading session. Some strategies, such as Distancing (personal connection questions), may more readily apply in some stories than others. Stories will also vary in the complexity of their plot, writing style, and vocabulary, which will affect how often you may use the Encourage vocabulary strategy, Open-ended questions, and Wh-questions.

As discussed in chapter 3, the most difficult strategies to use are Expanding on the child's response and encouraging Repetition. Adults should recognize that these will be difficult techniques for them to adopt and should try to use these more frequently as they progress through reading sessions with the child. One strategy that adults can aim to use every time, though, is the Make it fun technique!

Table 6.1 shows EMPOWERED strategies used while reading *Sylvester and the Magic Pebble* individually to three kindergarteners who were identified as at-risk for language and reading delays. As you can see, even with the same kindergartener, for example, Child A, different strategies are used across sessions 1, 2, and 3, as the adult and child progress through the story. When examining the pattern of

Table 6.1 EMPOWERED Strategy Usage for Three Kindergarteners While Reading *Sylvester and the Magic Pebble*

	E	M	P	O	W	E	R	E	D
Child A:									
Session 1	✓	✓	✓		✓		✓	✓	✓
Session 2	✓	✓	✓	✓			✓	✓	✓
Session 3	✓	✓	✓	✓	✓			✓	✓
Child B:									
Session 1	✓	✓	✓			✓		✓	✓
Session 2	✓		✓	✓	✓			✓	
Session 3	✓	✓	✓	✓	✓		✓	✓	✓
Child C:									
Session 1	✓	✓	✓			✓		✓	✓
Session 2	✓	✓	✓	✓	✓			✓	
Session 3	✓	✓	✓		✓			✓	✓
Session 4	✓	✓	✓	✓			✓	✓	✓

Note: E = Encourage Vocabulary; M = Make It Fun; P = Prompt Frequently; O = Open-ended Questions; W = Wh-questions; E = Expand; R = Encourage Repetition; E = Evaluate; D = Distancing.

strategies used with the three children, you can see that some strategies are frequently used, such as Encourage vocabulary, Make it fun, Prompt frequently, and Evaluate (i.e., praise and encouragement).

There is a little more variability in the use of Open-ended questions, Wh-questions, and Distancing questions, which as previously discussed, will depend on a number of factors related to the story as well as the child's age and receptiveness to the questions. Also, as previously discussed, the Expand and encourage Repetition strategies are used the least because they tend to be most difficult for adults to adopt.

Table 6.2 shows EMPOWERED strategies used while reading *The Patchwork Quilt* individually with at-risk first graders who had below-average reading comprehension. As you can see, the pattern of strategies is similar to the reading sessions with kindergarteners in table 6.1. Encourage vocabulary, Make it fun, Prompt frequently, and Evaluate are most frequently used, whereas Expanding on the child's responses and encouraging Repetition are the least frequently used strategies.

Lastly, table 6.3 presents EMPOWERED strategies used with two children. One was a second grader who had expressive language impairment and reading delays. He was participating in DRIVE reading

Table 6.2   EMPOWERED Strategy Usage for Three First Graders While Reading *The Patchwork Quilt*

	E	M	P	O	W	E	R	E	D
Child A:									
Session 1	✓	✓			✓				✓
Session 2	✓	✓	✓	✓	✓	✓	✓	✓	✓
Session 3	✓		✓		✓			✓	✓
Session 4	✓	✓	✓	✓	✓		✓	✓	✓
Session 5	✓	✓	✓	✓	✓	✓	✓	✓	✓
Child B:									
Session 1	✓	✓		✓		✓		✓	✓
Session 2	✓	✓		✓	✓				✓
Session 3	✓	✓	✓	✓	✓	✓	✓	✓	✓
Session 4	✓	✓	✓	✓	✓	✓	✓	✓	✓
Session 5	✓	✓	✓	✓	✓				✓
Child C:									
Session 1	✓	✓	✓	✓	✓	✓	✓	✓	✓
Session 2	✓	✓		✓	✓			✓	✓
Session 3	✓	✓	✓	✓	✓		✓	✓	✓
Session 4	✓	✓		✓	✓	✓	✓	✓	✓
Session 5	✓	✓	✓	✓	✓	✓	✓		✓

Note: E = Encourage Vocabulary; M = Make It Fun; P = Prompt Frequently; O = Open-ended Questions; W = Wh-questions; E = Expand; R = Encourage Repetition; E = Evaluate; D = Distancing.

sessions as an intervention to improve his reading comprehension and vocabulary. The other child was a third grader who participated in DRIVE sessions as an enrichment.

The top portion of table 6.3 shows three weekly sessions of about thirty minutes each in which an adult read *The Principal's New Clothes* by Stephanie Calmenson to the second grader. This book was read in weeks one through three of a nine-week individual intervention. The child was initially very reluctant to answer questions, and when he did, he responded with one-word answers. Therefore, the goal of these initial intervention sessions was to keep the mood light, engage him in the stories, and make reading a fun experience.

As you can see, Making it fun and using Open-ended and Wh-questions were the primary EMPOWERED strategies used. Expanding on the child's responses to model more complex language was also a primary technique. During the reading of this book, the adult did not emphasize requesting Repetition of expanded language. However, this

Table 6.3 EMPOWERED Strategy Usage for a Second Grader and Third Grader

	E	M	P	O	W	E	R	E	D
Second Grader[a]									
Session 1		✓	✓	✓	✓	✓			
Session 2	✓	✓	✓	✓	✓	✓			✓
Session 3	✓	✓		✓	✓	✓			✓
Third Grader[b]									
Session 1	✓	✓	✓		✓	✓		✓	
Session 2	✓	✓	✓	✓	✓	✓	✓	✓	✓
Session 3	✓	✓		✓	✓	✓		✓	
Session 4	✓	✓	✓	✓	✓	✓	✓	✓	✓
Session 5	✓	✓	✓	✓	✓	✓	✓	✓	

Note: E = Encourage Vocabulary; M = Make It Fun; P = Prompt Frequently; O = Open-ended Questions; W = Wh-questions; E = Expand; R = Encourage Repetition; E = Evaluate; D = Distancing.
[a] *The Principal's New Clothes*
[b] *Magic Tree House: Dinosaurs before Dark*

became a more frequent technique in subsequent sessions (not shown in the table) as the child became more comfortable with the back-and-forth questioning and dialogue.

The bottom portion of table 6.3 shows five weekly individual sessions of about thirty minutes each, in which an adult read the chapter book *The Magic Tree House: Dinosaurs before Dark* by Mary Pope Osborne to a third grader as enrichment while the child was attending school remotely during the COVID-19 pandemic. This student was very eager to read with the adult and was enthusiastic about engaging in a conversation about the story. As you can see, almost all of the EMPOWERED strategies were used at every reading session. Even with a very motivated child, it is apparent that not all of the strategies are used all of the time because the types of strategies used will depend on what is happening in the story at any point in time.

TYPES OF QUESTIONS

The DRIVE approach emphasizes the use of Open-ended questions which will encourage children to provide more than a one-word answer. This approach also involves asking Wh-questions that are also open-ended, such as "Where do you think the character is going?" Open-ended and Wh-questions are an essential part of dialogic reading because they promote comprehension of the story and encourage children to develop more complex language. If adults only asked closed-ended questions which yield a yes/no answer or a one-word response, children would not be able to develop more sophisticated oral language during dialogic reading sessions.

As discussed in chapter 3, there are times when it is appropriate to use closed-ended (or structured) questions. For very young children, those who are learning English as a second language, or children who are initially reluctant to respond to questioning, it is acceptable to begin by asking closed-ended questions when using the DRIVE approach. Examples of closed-ended Wh-questions would be "What is that?" or "What do you see on this page?" Just remember to transition to more open-ended questions and slowly phase out closed-ended questions as the child becomes more comfortable with engaging in a dialogue.

SCAFFOLDING

There are specific times when adults need to use scaffolding techniques to help the child participate in a dialogue or come to an understanding of a new vocabulary word. Scaffolding refers to any type of temporary support that helps children accomplish a variety of tasks that may be challenging at first.

Scaffolding can be used when discussing new vocabulary words in a story. If a child does not know the meaning of a word when asked, do not allow random guessing. Instead, provide the child with an appropriate scaffold to help them reach an understanding of the word.

One way to scaffold vocabulary might be with a Distancing prompt. For example, in *Earthquack!* by Margie Palatini the main character, Little Chucky Ducky, repeatedly shouts "The earth is crumbling!" to warn his friends of an earthquake. When introducing the meaning of the word *crumbling*, you could use a Distancing prompt by asking the child what would happen if they squeezed a cookie or muffin in their hand. The child might respond that the cookie would break into little pieces. You could then relate this back to the earth crumbling and ask the child to explain what the word means in the story.

An additional way to scaffold vocabulary is to use gestures, movements, or mime yourself or encourage the child to use these behaviors to show you what the word means. Chapter 2 discussed using movements to help the child understand the word *stomping*, where you first ask the child to show you the action and then ask them to use words to describe what they did.

Another example would be to use gestures to hint at the meaning of the word *wondering*. You might say to the child "Hmm. I'm wondering if they will have chicken nuggets for lunch in the cafeteria," while looking upward and tapping your chin. Then ask the child what wondering means in this context and tie it back to how *wondering* is used in the story with "Now tell me what does wondering mean?"

After you have attempted to scaffold the child's understanding of a vocabulary word, do not worry if they still are not able to verbalize what the word means. Remember that children need to encounter a word and use it many times in order to take ownership of its meaning.[1] As discussed in chapter 4, it is acceptable to provide a definition of the word in a way that the child understands, and ask them to tell you what it means (encourage Repetition).

WAIT TIME FOR RESPONSES

When asking questions, be patient. Wait about three seconds after asking a question to give the child time to formulate a response. Increasing wait time after asking a question increases the quality of the child's response and can encourage further language and vocabulary development, especially for children learning a second language.[2] If the child doesn't respond to your question, or if the child doesn't provide a "good" answer, do not give the answer. Instead, scaffold the response by providing hints or clues, modifying the question, or by re-reading.

There is no rule that you absolutely must wait three seconds. The ideal length of wait time will depend on the child's age and developmental level, attention span, and your own comfort level. Some experts also recommend that you begin with a one-second pause and gradually increase it to three seconds.[3] Using social-emotional cues, such as eye contact, a smile, and a pleasant facial expression, can also convey a positive atmosphere during the dialogic reading session, which may encourage children to become more comfortable taking time to formulate a response.

HANDLING DISTRACTIONS

Sometimes you might find that a child is distracted during shared reading. There are several EMPOWERED strategies that you can use to help the child to refocus. One strategy, which has been mentioned before, is to allow children to demonstrate new vocabulary words by moving around, gesturing, or miming. Anything you can do to Make it fun will also go a long way toward keeping children engaged in the story.

Another good way is to use a Distancing prompt to have the child make a personal connection related to the story. This gives the child an opportunity to talk about something they are familiar with, and it gives them a break from focusing on the story. Once the child is re-engaged, you can then lure them back to focusing on the story using the connection you have made. For example, when reading *Miss Nelson Is Missing*, asking the child whether they have had a substitute teacher (a very likely scenario) is an easy Distancing prompt. You can then take their experience with a substitute and tie it back to the children in the story.

USE PICTURES JUDICIOUSLY

The original dialogic reading approach suggests that adults ask questions about objects or pictures. This was reflected in the completion prompt strategy (the C in the acronym CROWD) and the P in the PEER acronym reminding adults to prompt children to label objects or discuss the story.[4] Examples of this strategy are: "When Sammy went outside, she put on ___?" or "What is this called?" (pointing to an object). Relying on pictures is appropriate for young children (ages two and three), and even the researchers who developed the original dialogic reading approach suggest separate approaches for two- to three-year-olds and four- to five-year-olds where simpler questions are asked of younger children.[5]

When using DRIVE with primary school children, remember to use pictures judiciously because the goal is for them to derive meaning from the text and from the adult-child interactions. For children who initially may be reluctant to engage in dialogue, it is acceptable to occasionally ask them to label objects or identify pictures in addition to asking structured questions (those for which there is a single answer), as discussed earlier. However, as children become more comfortable with the dialogue, it is important to transition away from using pictures to more open-ended questions that promote comprehension of the story and development of language skills.

There are a few instances, though, where using pictures in the story can be helpful in supporting vocabulary and comprehension.

- When beginning a new book, adults can use the picture on the cover to introduce the story using strategies such as Open-ended questions, Wh-questions, and Distancing questions. You might ask who the characters shown in the picture might be, what activity is being illustrated, whether the child has participated in the activity shown on the cover or similar types of activities, and what the child thinks the story might be about based on the title of the story and the cover picture.
- Pictures can also be used as a scaffold to help the child understand the meaning of a new vocabulary word in the story. For example, in *Doctor DeSoto* by William Steig, the word *wailed* in the sentence *"Please!' the fox wailed"* will be unfamiliar to most children. Adults can Encourage vocabulary by using the picture showing the fox with tears running down his face. Using what children know about crying and tears, adults can help them understand that wailing is a form of crying that involves intense emotion related to feelings of pain, grief, or anger.

While pictures can be used sparingly to engage the child in dialogue about the story, pictures should *not* be used as a strategy to help a child identify an unknown word while reading. Teachers sometimes encourage young readers to use a picture, which represents the meaning of the text on a page, to help identify an unknown word.[6] They also sometimes instruct students to identify an unfamiliar word using strategies such as asking "Does it sound right?" (testing whether the word fits the sentence grammatically) or "Does it make sense?" (testing whether the word makes sense within the context of the meaning of the sentence).[7]

For very early readers, these types of context cues can be beneficial but only when used after a reader attempts to decode, or sound out, an unfamiliar word as a way to confirm whether the attempt is correct. That is, using context in the form of looking at pictures or asking whether an attempted word sounds right and makes sense should be a secondary strategy to evaluate the accuracy of the child's attempt to decode an unknown word rather than the primary strategy for identifying unknown words.[8]

There is a body of research showing that relying on context cues to predict or guess at unknown words will not lead children to become proficient readers.[9,10] Use of contextual cues rather than relying on automatic word recognition and decoding is a characteristic of poor readers. On the other hand, proficient readers use decoding as a primary strategy when reading unfamiliar words.[11,12]

So, remember that the rule of thumb is to use pictures sparingly when creating a dialogue about the story. Questions about pictures can be used with very young children and as an initial strategy with struggling readers who are hesitant to engage in dialogue. They can also be used to introduce the story, as when discussing the book cover using Open-ended, Wh-questions, or Distancing questions, as well as to support the comprehension of a vocabulary word within the story. However, pictures should not be used as a strategy to identify or guess at unknown words while reading.

MAKE IT FUN

The advice to have fun was a recommendation in the original dialogic reading approach.[13] You may recall from chapter 3 that this advice has become part of the DRIVE approach. The M in the EMPOWERED acronym of strategies, stands for Make it fun. The child should feel that reading is a pleasure, not a chore. Adults do not need to stop at every page to ask a question, and they may ask several questions about the same page. This decision depends on how much text is on a page and at what points in the story it seems appropriate to stop and discuss. If a child appears to be getting bored or annoyed by the question-asking, move on. Always keep the mood light and convey your joy of reading.

WORK INDIVIDUALLY

The original research on dialogic reading was implemented in small groups at preschools and individually with parents.[14] However, for optimal results, individual DRIVE sessions are recommended over small groups especially when working with struggling readers in the primary grades.[15] The larger the student-to-adult ratio, the fewer opportunities for dialogue each child will have. Within a small-group format, it is difficult to control the attention of each student and the adult can only ask a question of one student at a time. Therefore, students must conform to the expectation of "sit and be quiet" which contradicts the objective of the approach.[16]

Teachers, paraprofessionals, librarians, and other educators will obviously need to implement the DRIVE approach with groups of children. In this case, a group size of five or fewer is recommended.[17] Adults will need to make other minor adjustments in the approach for a group format. The next section provides specific tips for this purpose.

SPECIAL TIPS FOR EDUCATORS AND LIBRARIANS

Depending on the nature of the group setting, educators, and librarians may need to adjust the type of book that is chosen. You may need to choose shorter books that can be finished within a single session, especially in library "story hour" where there may be different groups of children from week to week. However, reading longer books over multiple sessions (as the technique was intended) may work in other settings such as a library "book club" or in a classroom setting.

For multiple, short sessions with a lengthier book, you can begin and end a session with two book-end questions. At the beginning of the session, a good Wh-question to begin with is "What happened last time in the story?" This will prompt recall and is a good way to begin the dialogue. You might also ask about particularly important vocabulary words, especially those that repeat throughout the story to aid understanding. At the end of the session, you can ask a prediction question such as "What do you think will happen next?" encouraging the children to think about what they have already read and link it to what might be coming.

When working with a group of children, implementing some of the EMPOWERED strategies may be more challenging than when working with an individual child. But the strategies can be adapted for small groups keeping a couple of points in mind. One of the more challenging strategies (even when working with individual children) is encouraging Repetition. With a small group of children, this strategy might work best as a choral response, "Let's all say it together." This will ensure that all children are engaged, even the ones who are hesitant to answer individually, and it may also contribute to Making it fun.

When using Distancing prompts and Wh-questions working with a group, you may find that the same child (or children) are always responding. This is similar to what educators may face in the classroom. Additionally, the adult reader may not be able to provide scaffolding tailored to the level of each individual child.[18] Being aware of including all children is an obvious, important first step. However, you can also use responses to Distancing prompts and Wh-questions from a given child to prompt another child.

Using *The Patchwork Quilt* as an example, if one child responds that they know what a quilt is because their grandmother made them one, you might ask if anyone else has a quilt on their bed (or something other than a quilt). Or when Encouraging vocabulary, you might ask several children to respond first regarding the meaning of a word (this will encourage a more complete definition and contribute to each child's understanding of the word). Then it is important to have the whole group repeat back the meaning of the word together (encourage Repetition).

One final consideration when working with a small group of children concerns giving children adequate time to respond to a question or prompt. Remember that while there is not a specific rule for how long you should wait for a response, when working with an individual child a wait time of about three seconds is recommended. With a group of children, you may need to adjust this wait time. Waiting too long may lead to off-task behavior, especially for children who have not been asked the question.

In a younger group of children who may have shorter attention spans, a lengthy wait time may distract children from the book and hinder comprehension of the story.[19] While you want to make sure to be patient and allow children time to respond, you may need to decrease wait time. Again, this will be dependent on the group and factors such as age and whether many (or most) of the children in the group are interested and engaged in the story.

SUMMARY

Whether you are working with an individual child or a small group of children, using the EMPOWERED strategies outlined in chapter 3 together with the tips highlighted here, you can create a shared reading experience that will aid both comprehension and vocabulary development. While it is important to plan ahead and choose books that have an engaging story as well as a rich vocabulary in order to implement DRIVE, it is equally important to keep the reading sessions enjoyable. Making it fun will get children excited about reading and motivated to read in other settings beyond the DRIVE sessions. Chapter 7 will present some final thoughts as well as provide some additional resources for you.

NOTES

1. Barbara A. Wasik, Annemarie H. Hindman, and Emily K. Snell. "Book Reading and Vocabulary Development: A Systematic Review." *Early Childhood Research Quarterly* 37 (2016): 39–57. doi: 10.1016/j.ecresq.2016.04.003.
2. Barbara A. Wasik and Annemarie H. Hindman. "Why Wait? The Importance of Wait Time in Developing Young Students' Language and Vocabulary Skills." *Reading Teacher* 72, no. 3 (2018): 369–378. doi: 10.1002/trtr.1730.
3. Ibid.
4. Andrea Zevenbergen and Grover Whitehurst. "Dialogic Reading: A Shared Picture Book Intervention for Preschoolers." In *On Reading Books to Children: Parents and Teachers*, ed. Anne van Kleek, Steven Stahl and Eurydice Bauer (Mahwah, NJ: Lawrence Erlbaum Associates, 2003), 177–220.
5. Ibid.
6. Kerry Hempenstall. Education News. *The Three-Cueing Model: Down for the Count?* 2006. www.ednews.org/articles/4084/The-three-cueing-model--Down-for-the-count/Page1.html.
7. Ibid.
8. Dennis S. Davis, Jill S. Jones, and Courtney Samuelson. "Is It Time for a Hard Conversation about Cueing Systems and Word Reading in Teacher Education?" *Reading and Writing Quarterly* 37, no. 4 (2021): 301–316. doi: 10.1080/10573569.2020.1792813.

9. Linnea Ehri. "Orthographic Mapping and Literacy Development Revisited." In *Theories of Reading Development*, ed. Kate Cain, Donald Compton, and Rauno Parrila. (Philadelphia, PA: John Benjamins, 2017), 127–146.

10. Barbara Foorman et al. *Foundational Skills to Support Reading for Understanding in Kindergarten Through 3rd Grade (NCEE 2016-4008)* (Washington, DC: National Center for Education Evaluation and Regional Assistance (NCEE), Institute of Education Sciences, U.S. Department of Education, 2016). Retrieved from the NCEE website: http://whatworks.ed.gov.

11. Katherine Miles and Linnea Ehri. "Orthographic Mapping Facilitates Sight Word Memory and Vocabulary Learning." In *Reading Development and Difficulties: Bridging the Gap Between Research and Practice* (Cham, Switzerland: Springer, 2019), 63–82.

12. Mark Seidenberg. *Language at the Speed of Sight: How We Read, Why So Many Can't, and What Can Be Done About It* (New York: Basic Books, 2017).

13. David H. Arnold, Christopher J. Lonigan, Grover J. Whitehurst, and Jeffery N. Epstein. "Accelerating Language Development Through Picture Book Reading: Replication and Extension to a Videotape Training Format." *Journal of Educational Psychology* 86, no. 2 (1994): 235–243.

14. Grover J. Whitehurst, David S. Arnold, Jeffery N. Epstein, Andrea L. Angell, Meagan Smith, and Janet E. Fischel. "A Picture Book Reading Intervention in Day Care and Home for Children from Low-Income Families." *Developmental Psychology* 30, no. 5 (1994): 679–689.

15. Robert M. Schwartz, Maribeth C. Schmitt, and Mary K. Lose. "Effects of Teacher-Student Ratio in Response to Intervention Approaches." *The Elementary School Journal* 112, no. 4 (2012): 547–567. doi: 10.1360/zd-2013-43-6-1064.

16. Whitehurst et al., "A Picture Book Reading Intervention in Day Care and Home for Children from Low-Income Families."

17. Grover J. Whitehurst, Jeffrey N. Epstein, Andrea L. Angell, Adam C. Payne, Deanne A. Crone, and Janet E. Fischel. "Outcomes of an Emergent Literacy Intervention in Head Start." *Journal of Educational Psychology* 86, no. 4 (1994): 542–555.

18. Christopher Lonigan, Jason L. Anthony, Brenlee G. Bloomfield, Sarah M. Dyer, and Corine S. Samwel. "Effects of Two Shared-Reading Interventions on Emergent Literacy Skills of At-Risk Preschoolers." *Journal of Early Intervention* 22, no. 4 (1999): 306–322.

19. Wasik and Hindman. "Why Wait? The Importance of Wait Time in Developing Young Students' Language and Vocabulary Skills."

Chapter 7

Closing Thoughts

By now, you have a good idea about how to use the DRIVE approach with its EMPOWERED strategies to read with young children and school-age children in a variety of settings. Maybe you have already tried the DRIVE approach while reading some of the earlier chapters. But if you haven't, now is your chance to put your new knowledge and skills to work.

If you are still hesitant to try this dialogic reading approach, it is important to remember that there is no perfect way to do it. The sample dialogues in chapter 3 and the examples provided throughout the book are merely suggestions. When planning to read a story, there are:

- many different points in the story where you could decide to stop and ask questions (Prompt frequently);
- many possible Open-ended questions and Wh-questions you can think of;
- probably more potential vocabulary words to choose than you could possibly discuss; and
- many ways that a conversation can turn depending on the child's responses to Open-ended questions, Wh-questions, and Distancing questions.

Therefore, it is likely that when using the DRIVE approach while reading the same book, to several children, no two dialogues will be exactly alike. And that is by design. In fact, in research where undergraduate students have read to K-2 children in schools, they do read the same book individually to different children. And no two dialogues are identical. Children will have different levels of background knowledge, vocabulary, interests, and motivation.

Because the specific questions and techniques used in the DRIVE approach will vary from child to child, planning is key, as discussed in chapter 5. But you should not feel as though you need to stick to a script or prepare a lesson. For example, the sample prompts shown in table 7.1 as suggested questions for reading parts of *Sylvester and the Magic Pebble* are just that, samples. They are not meant to be a prescription for what questions you should use while reading. Rather, they are provided to give you an idea of where to start.

For a book like *Sylvester and the Magic Pebble* which is a longer picture book that contains quite a bit of text and content, it may seem easier to use the EMPOWERED strategies. However, as noted in chapter 5, shorter books with less text but that have an interesting and engaging story can also generate a rich dialogue. *Hello Lighthouse* discussed in chapter 3 is a good example of a shorter book with rich dialogue. Another is *A Most Unusual Day* by Sydra Mallery, a book about a young girl's day as she waits for her parents to bring home a newly adopted baby.

Table 7.2 gives a sample script for parts of *A Most Unusual Day*. As you can see from the sample script, there are many opportunities to use the EMPOWERED strategies. This story will also generate lots of different dialogues depending on the child's background and family life, allowing for individualized questions as you proceed with the story. While you may have planned ahead before reading with a child, you also will need to be able to be spontaneous on occasion.

FINAL ADVICE

Even when you have carefully planned what questions to ask, where to stop, and what vocabulary words to focus on, it is okay if the dialogic reading session does not go as expected. There is room for improvising the techniques while reading. That is why you may remember a frequent recommendation throughout the book to "take your cues from the child."

Table 7.1 Sample Script Using EMPOWERED Strategies for Reading *Sylvester and the Magic Pebble* by William Steig

Sample Prompts	Strategy
Showing the inside photo after the cover: • Who do you think this is? (Sylvester) • What is he holding? (a pebble) • What is a pebble? (a small rock)	• <u>P</u>rompt frequently • Ask a <u>W</u>h-question about the cover
After reading the first page: • Who does Sylvester live with? (his parents) • What does Sylvester like to do, what is his hobby? (Collecting pebbles of all shapes and colors) • Do you have a hobby?	• <u>P</u>rompt frequently • Ask <u>O</u>pen-ended <u>W</u>h-questions • Ask an <u>O</u>pen-ended <u>D</u>istancing question
After reading the second page: • What did Sylvester find? (a red pebble) • The pebble was remarkable. What does remarkable mean? • Continue dialogue	• <u>P</u>rompt frequently • Ask a <u>W</u>h-question • Ask an <u>E</u>ncourage vocabulary question • Follow up response with <u>E</u>xpansion, encourage <u>R</u>epetition, <u>E</u>valuate
• Sylvester wished it would stop raining. What do you think will happen next? After reading the third page: • What happened to the rain? (it stopped) • The clouds disappeared. What does disappear mean? • Continue dialogue	• Ask an <u>O</u>pen-ended <u>W</u>h-question (prediction) • <u>P</u>rompt frequently • Ask a <u>W</u>h-question • Ask an <u>E</u>ncourage vocabulary question • Follow up response with <u>E</u>xpansion, <u>E</u>ncourage <u>R</u>epetition, <u>E</u>valuate

. . .

Resuming on a different day: • Remind me, what happened in the story up to this point? After reading the seventh page: • What did Sylvester wish for? (to be a rock) • Right, Sylvester panicked and wished he was a rock. What does panicked mean? • Continue dialogue	• Ask an <u>O</u>pen-ended <u>W</u>h-question (recall) • <u>P</u>rompt frequently • Ask a <u>W</u>h-question • Ask an <u>E</u>ncourage vocabulary question • Follow up response with <u>E</u>xpansion, encourage <u>R</u>epetition, <u>E</u>valuate

(Continued)

Table 7.1   Continued

Sample Prompts	Strategy
• Why was the lion puzzled? What does that mean? • Continue dialogue	• <u>W</u>h-question, <u>E</u>ncourage vocabulary question • Follow up response with <u>E</u>xpansion, encourage <u>R</u>epetition, <u>E</u>valuate
After reading the ninth page: • How would you feel if you were Sylvester?	• Prompt frequently • Ask an <u>O</u>pen-ended, <u>D</u>istancing question
. . . Now you try it!	

Remember that DRIVE is an evidence-based approach, meaning that its development was based on a body of research regarding the benefits of dialogic reading for reading outcomes such as vocabulary and comprehension. What you now have at your disposal is a set of specific techniques, which you can use as tools to guide you in creating engaging dialogues with children while reading. Consistent use of the EMPOWERED strategies over time will yield the best results.

ADDITIONAL RESOURCES

For those who would like to learn more about how to encourage children to become good readers, next you will find helpful resources, such as books, reader-friendly articles, websites, and video clips.

Books

There are several reader-friendly books that are recommended for caregivers and educators which focus on different components of learning to read that were discussed in chapter 1.

For anyone who reads to young children, a good companion to this book would be another book written by one of the current authors, Dina Moore. This book entitled *Preparing Children for Reading Success: Hands-On Activities for Librarians, Educators, and Caregivers* and coauthored by senior research scientist at Haskins Laboratories, Julia Irwin, is designed to promote early literacy in young children from infancy to kindergarten.

Closing Thoughts

Table 7.2 Sample Script Using EMPOWERED Strategies for Reading *A Most Unusual Day* by Sydra Mallery

Sample Prompts	Strategy
Starting with the cover and title: • This book is called A Most Unusual Day • Do you know what unusual means? • Continue dialogue	• <u>P</u>rompt frequently • Ask an <u>E</u>ncourage vocabulary question • Follow up response with <u>E</u>xpansion, encourage <u>R</u>epetition, <u>E</u>valuate
After reading the first page: • What do you usually do when you first wake up? After reading the second page: • There's the word unusual again, do you remember what unusual means? • Continue dialogue	• <u>P</u>rompt frequently • Ask an <u>O</u>pen-ended <u>D</u>istancing question • <u>P</u>rompt frequently • Ask an <u>E</u>ncourage vocabulary question • Follow up response with <u>E</u>xpansion, encourage <u>R</u>epetition, <u>E</u>valuate
After reading the third and fourth pages: • Have you ever had a day like Caroline's? . . .	• <u>P</u>rompt frequently • Ask an <u>O</u>pen-ended <u>D</u>istancing question
After reading the sixth page: • Let's look at this picture. Caroline is using her broccoli to make a family. See there is the mother, father, and Caroline. But she added one more thing, a little pea. • What do you think the pea is? (A little baby) . . .	• <u>P</u>rompt frequently • Ask an <u>O</u>pen-ended <u>W</u>h- question (prediction)
After reading the eighth page: • Do you know what graceful means? • What did Caroline do that wasn't graceful? (She bumped into her friend) • Continue dialogue • How would you feel if you were Caroline? • Continue dialogue	• <u>P</u>rompt frequently • Ask an <u>E</u>ncourage vocabulary question • Ask an <u>O</u>pen-ended <u>W</u>h- question • Follow up response with <u>E</u>xpansion, encourage <u>R</u>epetition, <u>E</u>valuate • Ask an <u>O</u>pen-ended <u>D</u>istancing question • Follow up response with <u>E</u>xpansion, encourage <u>R</u>epetition, <u>E</u>valuate

. . .

(Continued)

Table 7.2 Continued

Sample Prompts	Strategy
After reading the tenth page: • Caroline's dad said that they would be needing her help soon. What do you think they will need her help with? • If child isn't sure or doesn't respond, use the picture on bottom of page where Caroline is practicing holding and feeding a doll	• Prompt frequently • Ask an Open-ended, Wh- question
. . . Now you try it!	

The topics addressed include important pre-literacy skills such as alphabet knowledge, concepts about print, book handling skills, phonological awareness, and expressive vocabulary. For each of these skills, the authors provide step-by-step descriptions of evidence-based activities to do with a child or group of children to support these critical skills. The activities are also paired with specific children's books to complete the activities.

Researcher Mark Seidenberg's book, *Language at the Speed of Sight: How We Read, Why So Many Can't, and What Can be Done about It*, explains how learning to read is unique and very different from developing oral language. His book describes the science behind reading in an approachable way for educators of all levels as well as caregivers interested in deepening their knowledge of this topic beyond what has been covered in chapter 1 of this book.

The book begins by describing the history behind the relationships between speech, writing, and reading. Seidenberg then masterfully explains how we go about the process of reading, from eye movements to cognitive and brain processes to development of reading skills and reading disability. In the final section of the book, Seidenberg tackles how reading is taught in schools.

Natalie Wexler is an education journalist whose book *The Knowledge Gap: The Hidden Cause of America's Broken Education System—and How to Fix It* focuses on the singular message that individuals need background knowledge (also called prior knowledge) in order to understand the text that they read. This book also explains how reading is typically taught in many schools, some of the problems with common instructional approaches, and how we can improve reading instruction moving forward. This is a welcome resource for parents and caregivers of school-age children as well as teachers.

Daniel Willingham is a professor of psychology and author of the best-selling book, *Why Don't Students Like School?* In his book *Raising Kids Who Read: What Parents and Teachers Can Do*, Willingham provides general research-based recommendations for promoting the development of children's decoding and reading comprehension and encouraging their motivation to read. He takes a developmental approach by focusing on the needs of children from birth through preschool, those in the primary grades (K-2), and students in third grade and beyond.

While other books have focused on recommendations for improving skills like decoding and comprehension, Willingham provides a unique perspective in emphasizing the importance of motivation in becoming a good reader. Caregivers will find this book beneficial for increasing enthusiasm for reading in children of all ages.

Articles, Websites, and Videos

Reader-friendly articles can be informative resources for busy parents, caregivers, and educators. In the blog and online article below, renowned researcher and literacy expert, Louisa Moats, describes "the science of reading," which is an understanding of the reading process and reading acquisition based on decades of accumulated data from various disciplines. For those who would like to learn more about the reading skills discussed in chapter 1 of this book, these resources are a great place to start.

In these resources, Moats also elaborates on the need for research-based literacy instruction and improved teacher training. These sources provide important insights for educators of all levels.

- Collaborative Classroom. (2021). A conversation about the science of reading and early reading instruction with Dr. Louisa Moats. https://www.collaborativeclassroom.org/blog/the-science-of-reading-with-dr-louisa-moats/.
- Moats, L. C. (2020, Summer). Teaching reading is rocket science: What expert teachers of reading should know and be able to do. *American Educator*, *44*(2), 4–39. https://www.aft.org/sites/default/files/moats.pdf.

While it is important to understand what the science of reading is, it is just as critical to be aware of what it is not. Consistent with the science of reading, chapter 1 discusses how children learn to read new words through decoding and orthographic mapping. Contrary to the science of reading, many children are taught to read words through an approach called three-cueing. The two online articles listed below provide an easy-to-understand explanation of this three-cueing approach, which is *not* evidence-based and contradicts the science of reading.

- Five from Five. (2021). The three cueing system. https://fivefromfive.com.au/the-three-cueing-system/.
- Vaites, K. (2019, October). The trouble with common word recognition strategies. https://eduvaites.org/2019/10/21/the-trouble-with-common-word-recognition-strategies/.

Additionally, below are two websites from two reading experts that parents, caregivers, and educators at all levels might find helpful.

- Mark Seidenberg's website, Reading Matters: https://seidenbergreading.net/seidenblog/.

  Mark Seidenberg was mentioned earlier for his book, *Language at the Speed of Sight: How We Read, Why So Many Can't, and What Can Be Done about It*. His website hosts a variety of resources, including blogs, videos, an online book club, and many resources on "the science of reading." Because space in this book is limited, it would not be possible to list all reputable resources. So, Seidenberg's website is a great place to start.
- Timothy Shanahan's website, Shanahan on Literacy: https://www.shanahanonliteracy.com/.

  Timothy Shanahan, an emeritus professor and literacy expert, provides extensive resources on his website, including downloadable publications on the science of reading and blog posts on many reading topics.

Watch these two video clips to hear some of the original researchers of dialogic reading discuss this approach. Remember that this dialogic reading approach was originally developed for children ages two to five years old.

- Dr. Grover Whitehurst—Dialogic Reading Video Series: https://youtu.be/k-XlbJuCi3c
- Dr. Christopher Lonigan—Research on Dialogic Reading: https://youtu.be/r2FLrq8YIyY

Recall that chapter 1 discussed orthographic mapping, the process by which phonemes of a spoken word, the spelling pattern of the written word, and the word's meaning become bound together as a unit, allowing children to quickly and accurately recognize and comprehend words. This nine-minute video presented by Lyn Stone provides an easy-to-understand explanation of orthographic mapping.

- Lyn Stone—Orthographic Mapping Explainer: https://youtu.be/KIuwKnZqJEQ

Resources for Obtaining Books

The local public library can provide families with endless possibilities to explore all different sorts of books and help children discover what interests them. Parents, educators, and librarians also can use the following resources for obtaining books for children, especially those who face socioeconomic adversity.

- Book Trust—National literacy program that provides books to children in Title 1 schools: https://www.booktrust.org/
- Dolly Parton's Imagination Library—Provides free books to children from birth through age five through funding shared by Dolly Parton and community partners. https://imaginationlibrary.com/
- First Book—a nonprofit organization that provides access to new books for children in need. https://firstbook.org/
- National Home Library Foundation—Provides grants to purchase books for libraries, schools, and other literacy programs. http://homelibraryfoundation.org/
- Kids Need to Read—Provides books to underfunded libraries, schools, and literacy programs. http://www.kidsneedtoread.org/

Bibliography

Aarnoutse, Cor and Jan van Leeuwe. "Relation Between Reading Comprehension, Vocabulary, Reading Pleasure, and Reading Frequency." *Educational Research and Evaluation* 4, no. 2 (1998): 143–166. doi: 10.1076/edre.4.2.143.6960.

Allard, Harry, and James Marshall. *Miss Nelson is Back*. Boston, MA: Houghton Mifflin, 1982.

———. *Miss Nelson is Missing*. Boston, MA: Houghton Mifflin, 1977.

Anderson, Richard, and William Nagy. "Word Meanings." In *Handbook Of Reading Research, Vol. 2*, edited by Rebecca Barr, Michael Kamil, Peter Mosenthal, and P. David Pearson, 690–724. Mahwah, NJ: Lawrence Erlbaum, 1991.

Andrews, Troy. *Trombone Shorty*. New York: Abrams Books for Young Readers, 2015.

Anglin, Jeremy M., George A. Miller, and Pamela C. Wakefield. "Vocabulary Development: A Morphological Analysis." *Monographs of the Society for Research in Child Development* 58, no. 10 (1993): i. doi: 10.2307/1166112.

Arnold, David H., Christopher J. Lonigan, Grover J. Whitehurst, and Jeffery N. Epstein. "Accelerating Language Development Through Picture Book Reading: Replication and Extension to a Videotape Training Format." *Journal of Educational Psychology* 86, no. 2 (1994): 235–43.

Barnes, Erica, and Jaime Puccioni. "Shared Book Reading and Preschool Children's Academic Achievement: Evidence from the Early Childhood Longitudinal Study—Birth Cohort." *Infant and Child Development* 26, no. 6 (2017): 1–20. doi: 10.1002/icd.2035.

Beck, Isabel, Margaret McKeown, and Linda Kucan. *Bringing Words to Life: Robust Vocabulary Instruction* New York: Guilford Press, 2002.

———. *Bringing Words to Life: Robust Vocabulary Instruction* (2nd ed.). New York: Guilford Press, 2013.
Biemiller, Andrew. "Teaching Vocabulary: Early, Direct, and Sequential." *American Educator* 25 (2001, Spring): 24–28, 47.
Blackall, Sophie. *Hello Lighthouse*. New York: Little, Brown and Company, 2018.
Blom-Hoffman, Jessica, Therese M. O'Neil-Pirozzi, and Joanna Cutting. "Read Together, Talk Together: The Acceptability of Teaching Parents to Use Dialogic Reading Strategies via Videotaped Instruction." *Psychology in the Schools* 43, no. 1 (2006): 71–78.
Bloom, Lois. *One Word At a Time: The Use of Single Word Utterances Before Syntax*. The Hague, The Netherlands: Mouton, 1973.
Bortfeld, Heather, James L. Morgan, Roberta Michnick Golinkoff, and Karen Rathbun. "Mommy and Me." *Psychological Science* 16, no. 4 (2005): 298–304. doi: 10.1111/j.0956-7976.2005.01531.x.
Bradley, Lynette, and Peter Bryant. *Rhyme and Reason In Reading and Spelling*. Ann Arbor, MI: University of Michigan Press, 1985.
Bradley, Lynette and Peter E. Bryant. "Categorizing Sounds and Learning to Read: A Causal Connection." *Nature* 301 (1983): 419–421.
Brett, Jan. *The Hat*. New York: G.P. Putnam's Sons Books, 1997.
Brown, Jeff. *Flat Stanley: His Original Adventure*. New York: Harper Collins, 2013.
Burton, Virginia Lee. *The Little House*. Boston, MA: Houghton Mifflin Company, 1942.
Calmenson, Stephanie. *The Principal's New Clothes*. New York: Scholastic, 1991.
Chard, David J., Sharon Vaughn, and Brenda-Jean Tyler. "A Synthesis of Research on Effective Interventions for Building Reading Fluency with Elementary Students with Learning Disabilities." *Journal of Learning Disabilities* 35, no. 5 (2002): 386–406.
Chiaraluce, Brianna. "Evaluating the Treatment Fidelity of a Dialogic Reading Intervention." Poster presented at the annual meeting of the Northeastern Educational Research Association, Trumbull, CT, October 2018.
Clement, Rod. *Grandpa's Teeth*. New York: Harper Collins, 1998.
Cline, Keely D., and Carolyn Pope Edwards. "Parent–Child Book-Reading Styles, Emotional Quality, and Changes in Early Head Start Children's Cognitive Scores." *Early Education and Development* 28, no. 1 (2017): 41–58. doi: 10.1080/10409289.2016.1177392.
Corpus, Jennifer Henderlong, and Mark R. Lepper. "The Effects of Person versus Performance Praise on Children's Motivation: Gender and Age as Moderating Factors." *Educational Psychology* 27, no. 4 (2007): 487–508. doi: 10.1080/01443410601159852.

Dahl, Roald. *The Enormous Crocodile.* New York: Puffin Books, 1978.

Davis, Dennis S., Jill S. Jones, and Courtney Samuelson. "Is It Time for a Hard Conversation about Cueing Systems and Word Reading in Teacher Education?" *Reading and Writing Quarterly* 37, no. 4 (2021): 301–16. doi: 10.1080/10573569.2020.1792813.

de Jong, Maria T., and Adriana G. Bus. "Quality of Book-Reading Matters for Emergent Readers: An Experiment with the Same Book in a Regular or Electronic Format." *Journal of Educational Psychology* 94, no. 1 (2002): 145–155.

De La Pena, Matt. *Carmela Full of Wishes.* New York: G.P. Putnam's Sons, 2018.

Diaz, Junot. *Islandborn.* New York: Dial Books for Young Readers, 2018.

DiCamillo, Kate. *Mercy Watson to the Rescue.* Somerville, MA: Candlewick Press, 2009.

———. *Louise, The Adventures of a Chicken.* New York: Joanna Cotler Books, 2008.

Dowdall, Nicholas, G. J. Melendez-Torres, Lynne Murray, Frances Gardner, Leila Hartford, and Peter J. Cooper. "Shared Picture Book Reading Interventions for Child Language Development: A Systematic Review and Meta-Analysis." *Child Development* 91, no. 2 (2020): e383–99. doi: 10.1111/cdev.13225.

Duff, Fiona, and Paula Clarke. "Practitioner Review: Reading Disorders: What Are the Effective Interventions and How Should They Be Implemented and Evaluated?" *Journal of Child Psychology and Psychiatry* 52, no. 1 (2011): 3–12.

Durwin, Cheryl, Deborah Carroll, and Dina Moore. "Dialogic Reading: A Theory-Based Approach to Early Reading Intervention in Urban Schools." Poster presented at the annual meeting of the Eastern Psychological Association, New York, NY, March 2016.

Durwin, Cheryl, Dina Moore, and Deborah Carroll. "Can a Brief Dialogic Reading Intervention Improve Listening Comprehension of At-Risk Kindergartners?" Paper at roundtable session of annual meeting of the American Educational Research Association, San Francisco, CA, April 2020. Conference Canceled, http://tinyurl.com/v6gx3dh.

Durwin, Cheryl, Dina Moore, Deborah Carroll, and Brianna Chiaraluce. "Efficacy of a Dialogic Reading Intervention for At-Risk Readers in Urban Schools." Paper presented at the annual meeting of the American Educational Research Association, New York, NY, April 2018.

Ehri, Linnea. "Orthographic Mapping and Literacy Development Revisited." In *Theories of Reading Development,* edited by Kate Cain, Donald Compton, and Rauno Parrila, 127–146. Philadelphia, PA: John Benjamins, 2017.

Ehri, Linnea C. "Orthographic Mapping in the Acquisition of Sight Word Reading, Spelling Memory, and Vocabulary Learning." *Scientific Studies of Reading* 18, no. 1 (2014): 5–21. doi: 10.1080/10888438.2013.819356.

Ehri, Linnea C., Simone R. Nunes, Steven A. Stahl, and Dale M. Willows. "Systematic Phonics Instruction Helps Students Learn to Read: Evidence from the National Reading Panel's Meta-Analysis." *Review of Educational Research* 71, no. 3 (2001): 393–447. doi: 10.3102/00346543071003393.

Faber, Carrie. "Replicating the Treatment Fidelity of POWERED Strategies in the Dialogic Reading with Integrated Vocabulary Enrichment Intervention." Poster presented at the annual meeting of the New England Psychological Association, Worcester, MA, November 2018.

Fenson, Larry, Philip S. Dale, J. Steven Reznick, Elizabeth Bates, Donna J. Thal, and J. Pethick Stephen. "Variability in Communicative Development." *Monographs of the Society for Research in Child Development* 59, no. 242 (1994).

Flournoy, Valerie. *The Patchwork Quilt.* New York: Dial Books for Young Readers, 1985.

Foorman, Barbara, Nicholas Beyler, Kelley Borradaile, Michael Coyne, Carolyn Denton, Joseph Dimino, Joshua Furgeson, et al. *Foundational Skills to Support Reading for Understanding in Kindergarten Through 3rd Grade (NCEE 2016-4008).* Washington, DC: National Center for Education Evaluation and Regional Assistance (NCEE), Institute of Education Sciences, U.S. Department of Education, 2016. Retrieved from the NCEE website: http://whatworks.ed.gov.

Ford-Connors, Evelyn, and Jeanne R. Paratore. "Vocabulary Instruction in Fifth Grade and Beyond: Sources of Word Learning and Productive Contexts for Development." *Review of Educational Research* 85, no. 1 (2015): 50–91.

Fuchs, Lynn S, Douglas Fuchs, Michelle K Hosp, and Joseph R Jenkins. "Oral Reading Fluency as an Indicator of Reading Competence: A Theoretical, Empirical, and Historical Analysis," *Scientific Studies of Reading* 5, no. 3 (2001): 239–256.

Furenes, May Irene, Natalia Kucirkova, and Adriana G. Bus. "A Comparison of Children's Reading on Paper Versus Screen: A Meta-Analysis." *Review of Educational Research* 91, no. 4 (2021): 483–517. doi: 10.3102/0034654321998074.

Gilkerson, Jill, Jeffrey A. Richards, Steven F. Warren, D. Kimbrough Oller, Rosemary Russo, and Betty Vohr. "Language Experience in the Second Year of Life and Language Outcomes in Late Childhood." *Pediatrics* 142, no. 4 (2018): e20174276. doi: 10.1542/peds.2017-4276.

Goldin-Meadow, Susan, Susan C. Levine, Larry V. Hedges, Janellen Huttenlocher, Stephen W. Raudenbush, and Steven L. Small. "New Evidence about

Language and Cognitive Development Based on a Longitudinal Study: Hypotheses for Intervention." *American Psychologist* 69, no. 6 (2014): 588–599.
Gottfried, Allen W., Jonah Schlackman, Adele Eskeles Gottfried, and Alma S. Boutin-Martinez. "Parental Provision of Early Literacy Environment as Related to Reading and Educational Outcomes Across the Academic Lifespan." *Parenting* 15, no. 1 (2015): 24–38. doi: 10.1080/15295192.2015.992736.
Gough, Philip, and William Tunmer. "Decoding, Reading, and Reading Disability." *Remedial and Special Education* 7, no. 1 (1986): 6–10.
Hazen, Barbara Shook. *The Knight Who Was Afraid of the Dark.* London: Diamond Books, 1998.
Hempenstall, Kerry. Education News. *The three-cueing model: Down for the count?* 2006. www.ednews.org/articles/4084/The-three-cueing-model--Down-for-the-count/Page1.html.
Higgins, Ryan. *We Don't Eat Our Classmates.* New York: Scholastic, 2018.
Hoff, Erika. "The Specificity of Environmental Influence: Socioeconomic Status Affects Early Vocabulary Development via Maternal Speech." *Child Development* 74, no. 5 (2003): 1368–78. doi: 10.1111/1467-8624.00612.
Hort, Lenny. *How Many Stars in the Sky?* New York: Scholastic, 2013.
Hulme, Charles, and Margaret Snowling. "Children's Reading Comprehension Difficulties: Nature, Causes, and Treatments." *Current DIrections in Psychological Science* 20, no. 3 (2011): 139–142.
Irwin, Julia, and Dina Moore. *Preparing Children For Reading Success: Hands-On Activities for Librarians, Educators, and Caregivers.* Lanham, MD: Rowman & Littlefield, 2014.
Johnson, C. J., and J. M. Anglin. "Qualitative Developments in the Content and Form of Children's Definitions." *Journal of Speech and Hearing Research* 38, no. 3 (1995): 612–29. doi: 10.1044/jshr.3803.612.
Kaesmann, Stephanie. "Evaluating Treatment Fidelity of EMPOWERED Strategies in a Kindergarten Dialogic Reading Intervention." Poster presented at the annual meeting of the Northeastern Educational Research Association, online, October 2021.
Kasza, Keiko. *The Wolf's Chicken Stew.* New York: G.P. Putnam's Sons, 1987.
Korat, Ofra, Adina Shamir, and Shani Heibal. "Expanding the Boundaries of Shared Book Reading: E-Books and Printed Books in Parent-Child Reading as Support for Children's Language." *First Language* 33, no. 5 (2013): 504–23. doi: 10.1177/0142723713503148.
Krull, Kathleen. *Wilma Unlimited: How Wilma Rudolph Became the World's Fastest Woman.* San Diego, CA: Harcourt Brace & Company, 1996.
Levickis, Penny, Sheena Reilly, Luigi Girolametto, Obioha C. Ukoumunne, and Melissa Wake. "Maternal Behaviors Promoting Language Acquisition in Slow-to-Talk Toddlers." *Journal of Developmental & Behavioral Pediatrics* 35, no. 4 (May 2014): 274–281. doi: 10.1097/DBP.0000000000000056.

Lonigan, Christopher J., Jason L. Anthony, Brenlee G. Bloomfield, Sarah M. Dyer, and Corine S. Samwel. "Effects of Two Shared-Reading Interventions on Emergent Literacy Skills of At-Risk Preschoolers." *Journal of Early Intervention* 22, no. 4 (1999): 306–22.

Lonigan, Christopher J., Timothy Shanahan, and Anne Cunningham. *Impact of Shared-Reading Interventions on Young Children's Early Literacy Skills.* Developing Early Literacy: Report of the National Early Literacy Panel, In Eunice Kennedy Shriver National Institute of Child Health and Human Develpment, NIH, DHHS, Washington, DC: U.S. Government Printing Office, 153–171, 2008.

Lonigan, Christopher J., and Grover J. Whitehurst. 1998. "Relative Efficacy of Parent and Teacher Involvement in a Shared-Reading Intervention for Preschool Children from Low-Income Backgrounds." *Early Childhood Research Quarterly* 13, no. 2 (1998): 263–90.

Lord, John Vernon. *The Giant Jam Sandwich.* New York: Houghton Mifflin Harcourt, 2018.

Mallery, Sydra. *A Most Unusual Day.* New York: Greenwillow Books, 2018.

McCloskey, Robert. *Blueberries for Sal.* New York: Viking Press, 1948.

McKeown, Margaret G. "Effective Vocabulary Instruction Fosters Knowing Words, Using Words, and Understanding How Words Work." *Language, Speech, and Hearing Services in Schools* 50, no. 4 (2019): 466–76. doi: 10.1044/2019_LSHSS-VOIA-18-0126.

McKeown, Margaret G., and Isabel Beck. "Taking Advantage of Read-Alouds to Help Children." In *On Reading Books to Children: Parents and Teachers,* edited by Anne van Kleek, Steven Stahl, and Eurydice Bauer, 159–176. Mahwah, NJ: Lawrence Erlbaum Associates, 2003.

McMurray, Bob. "Defusing the Childhood Vocabulary Explosion." *Science* 317, no. 5838 (2007): 631. doi: 10.1126/science.1144073.

Melzi, Gigliana, and Margaret Caspe. "Variations in Maternal Narrative Styles during Book Reading Interactions." *Narrative Inquiry* 15, no. 1 (2005): 101–25. doi: 10.1075/ni.15.1.06mel.

Miles, Katherine, and Linnea Ehri. "Orthographic Mapping Facilitates Sight Word Memory and Vocabulary Learning." In *Reading Development and Difficulties: Bridging the Gap Between Research and Practice,* 63–82. Cham, Switzerland: Springer, 2019.

Mol, Suzanne E., and Adriana G. Bus. "To Read or Not to Read: A Meta-Analysis of Print Exposure From Infancy to Early Adulthood." *Psychological Bulletin* 137, no. 2 (2011): 267–96. doi: 10.1037/a0021890.

Mol, Suzanne E., Adriana G. Bus, and Maria T. de Jong. "Interactive Book Reading in Early Education: A Tool to Stimulate Print Knowledge as Well as Oral Language." *Review of Educational Research* 79, no. 2 (2009): 979–1007. doi: 10.3102/0034654309332561.

Morris, Richard. *Bear Came Along.* New York: Little, Brown, and Company, 2019.
Morrow, Lesley, and Rebecca Brittain. "The Nature of Storybook Reading in the Elementary school: Current Practices." In *On Reading Books to Children: Parents and Teachers,* edited by Anne van Kleek, Steven Stahl, and Eurydice Bauer, 140–158. Mahwah, NJ: Lawrence Erlbaum Associates, 2003.
Munzer, Tiffany G., Alison L. Miller, Heidi M. Weeks, Niko Kaciroti, and Jenny Radesky. "Differences in Parent-Toddler Interactions with Electronic versus Print Books." *Pediatrics* 143, no. 4 (April 1, 2019). doi: 10.1542/peds.2018-2012.
Nagy, William E., and Richard C. Anderson. "How Many Words Are There in Printed School English?" *Reading Research Quarterly* 19, no. 3 (1984): 304–30. doi: 10.2307/747823.
Nagy, William E., Richard C. Anderson, and Patricia A. Herman. "Learning Word Meanings From Context During Normal Reading." *American Educational Research Journal* 24, no. 2 (1987): 237–70. doi: 10.3102/00028312024002237.
Nagy, William E., and Judith Scott. "Vocabulary Processes." In *Handbook of Reading Research,* edited by Michael Kamil, Peter Mosenthal, P. David Pearson, and Rebecca Barr, 269–284. Mahwah, NJ: Erlbaum, 2000.
National Early Literacy Panel. *Developing Early Literacy: Report of the National Early Literacy Panel.* Washington, DC: National Institute for Literacy, 2008.
National Reading Panel (U.S.). Report of the National Reading Panel: Teaching Children To Read: An Evidence-Based Assessment of the Scientific Research Literature on Reading and Its Implications for Reading Instruction: Reports of the Subgroups. Washington, D.C.: National Institute of Child Health and Human Development, National Institutes of Health, 2000.
Osborne, Mary Pope. *Magic Treehouse Dinosaurs before Dark.* New York: Random House, 1992.
Ouellette, Gene P. "What's Meaning Got to Do with It: The Role of Vocabulary in Word Reading and Reading Comprehension." *Journal of Educational Psychology* 98, no. 3 (2006): 554–66.
Palatini, Margie. *Earthquack!* New York: Simon & Schuster, 2005.
Parish-Morris, Julia, Neha Mahajan, Kathy Hirsh-Pasek, Roberta Michnick Golinkoff, and Molly Fuller Collins. "Once upon a Time: Parent-Child Dialogue and Storybook Reading in the Electronic Era." *Mind, Brain, and Education* 7, no. 3 (2013): 200–211. doi: 10.1111/mbe.12028.
Park, Barbara. *Junie B. Jones and the Stupid Smelly Bus.* New York: Random House, 1992.
Patall, Erika A., Harris Cooper, and Susan R. Wynn. "The Effectiveness and Relative Importance of Choice in the Classroom." *Journal of Educational*

Psychology 102, no. 4 (November 2010): 896–915. doi: 10.1037/a0019545.
Phythian-Sence, Caroline, and Richard Wagner. "Vocabulary Acquisition: A Primer." In *Vocabulary Acquisition: Implications for Reading Comprehension*, 1–14. New York: Guliford Press, 2007.
Piasta, Shayne B., Yaacov Petscher, and Laura M. Justice. "How Many Letters Should Preschoolers in Public Programs Know? The Diagnostic Efficiency of Various Preschool Letter-Naming Benchmarks for Predicting First-Grade Literacy Achievement." *Journal of Educational Psychology* 104, no. 4 (2012): 945–58. doi: 10.1037/a0027757.
Plourde, Lynn. *Spring's Sprung*. New York: Simon & Schuster Books for Young Readers, 2002.
———. *Summer's Vacation*. New York: Simon & Schuster Books for Young Readers, 2003.
———. *Wild Child*. New York: Aladdin Paperbacks, 2003.
———. *Winter Waits*. New York: Aladdin Paperbacks, 2001.
Pressley, Michael, and Richard Allington. *Reading Instruction That Works: The Case for Balanced Teaching, 4th ed.* New York: Guilford, 2014.
Price, Joseph, and Ariel Kalil. "The Effect of Mother–Child Reading Time on Children's Reading Skills: Evidence From Natural Within-Family Variation." *Child Development* 90, no. 6 (2019): e688–702. doi: 10.1111/cdev.13137.
Reeve, Johnmarshall, and Hyungshim Jang. "What Teachers Say and Do to Support Students' Autonomy during a Learning Activity." *Journal of Educational Psychology* 98, no. 1 (2006): 209–18. doi: 10.1037/0022-0663.98.1.209.
Richter, Anna, and Mary L. Courage. "Comparing electronic and paper storybooks for preschoolers: Attention, engagement, and recall." *Journal of Applied Developmental Psychology* 48 (2017): 92–102.
Romeo, Rachel R., Julia A. Leonard, Sydney T. Robinson, Martin R. West, Allyson P. Mackey, Meredith L. Rowe, and John D.E. Gabrieli. "Beyond the 30-Million-Word Gap: Children's Conversational Exposure Is Associated With Language-Related Brain Function." *Psychological Science* 29, no. 5 (2018): 700–710. doi: 10.1177/0956797617742725.
Rowe, Meredith L. "Decontextualized Language Input and Preschoolers' Vocabulary Development." *Seminars in Speech and Language* 34, no. 4 (2013): 260–66. doi: 10.1055/s-0033-1353444.
Roy, Ron. *A to Z Mysteries The Absent Author*. New York: Random House, 1997.
Rvachew, Susan, Kathrin Rees, Elizabeth Carolan, and Aparna Nadig. "Improving Emergent Literacy with School-based Shared Reading: Paper Versus ebooks." *International Journal of Child-Computer Interaction* 12 (2017): 24–29.
Rylant, Cynthia. *The Relatives Came*. New York: Bradbury Press, 1985.

Scarborough, Hollis. "Connecting Early Language and Literacy to Later Reading (Dis)abilities." In *Handbook for Research in Early Literacy*, edited by Susan Neuman and David Dickinson, 97–110. New York: Guilford Press, 2001.

Scarborough, Hollis. "Early Identifcation of Children At Risk for Reading Disabilities: Phonological Awareness and Some Other Promising Predictors." In *Specific Reading Disability: A View of the Spectrum*, edited by Bruce Shapiro, Pasquale Accardo, and Arnold Capute. Timonium, MD: York Press, 1998.

Scherer, Nancy J, and Lesley B Olswang. "Role of Mothers' Expansions in Stimulating Children's Language Production." *Journal of Speech and Hearing Research* 27, no. September (1984): 387–96.

Schwartz, Robert M., Maribeth C. Schmitt, and Mary K. Lose. "Effects of Teacher-Student Ratio in Response to Intervention Approaches." *The Elementary School Journal* 112, no. 4 (2012): 547–67. doi: 10.1360/zd-2013-43-6-1064.

Seidenberg, Mark. *Language at the Speed of Sight: How We Read, Why So Many Can't, and What Can Be Done About It*. New York: Basic Books, 2017.

Selden, George. *The Cricket in Times Square*. New York: Ariel Books, 1960.

Shankweiler, Donald, and Anne E. Fowler. "Questions People Ask about the Role of Phonological Processes in Learning to Read." *Reading and Writing* 17, no. 5 (2004): 483–515. doi:10.1023/B:READ.0000044598.81628.e6.

Snow, Catherine, Patton Tabors, and David Dickinson. "Language Development in the Preshool Years, edited by David Dickinson and Patton Tabors." In *Beginning Literacy With Language*. Baltimore, MD: Brookes, 2001.

Standiford, Natalie. *The Bravest Dog Ever: The True Story of Balto*. New York: Random House, 2003.

Stanovich, Keith. "Matthew Effects in Reading: Some Consequences of Individual Differences in the Acquisition of Literacy." *Reading Research Quarterly* 21 no 4 (1986): 360–407.

Steig, William. *Brave Irene*. New York: Farrar, Straus, and Giroux, 1986.

———. *Doctor De Soto*. New York: Farrar, Straus, and Giroux, 1982.

———. *Sylvester and the Magic Pebble*. New York: Windmill Books, 1969.

Stevens, Elizabeth A, Melodee A Walker, and Sharon Vaughn. "The Effects of Reading Fluency Interventions on the Reading Fluency and Reading Comprehension Performance of Elementary Students with Learning Disabilities: A Synthesis of the Research from 2001 to 2014." *Journal of Learning Disabilities* 50, no. 5 (2017): 576–90. doi: 10.1177/0022219416638028.

Stevens, Janet, and Susan Stevens Crummel. *The Donkey Egg*. New York: Houghton Mifflin Harcourt, 2019.

Suggate, Sebastian, Elizabeth Schaughency, Helena McAnally, and Elaine Reese. "From Infancy to Adolescence: The Longitudinal Links between Vocabulary, Early Literacy Skills, Oral Narrative, and Reading

Comprehension." *Cognitive Development* 47 (2018): 82–95. doi: 10.1016/j.cogdev.2018.04.005.

Swanson, Elizabeth, Sharon Vaughn, Jeanne Wanzek, Yaacov Petscher, Jennifer Heckert, Christie Cavanaugh, Guliz Kraft, and Kathryn Tackett. "A Synthesis of Read-Aloud Interventions on Early Reading Outcomes among Preschool through Third Graders at Risk for Reading Difficulties." *Journal of Learning Disabilities* 44, no. 3 (2011): 258–75. doi:10.1177/0022219410378444.

Takacs, Zsofia K., Elise K. Swart, and Adriana G. Bus. "Benefits and Pitfalls of Multimedia and Interactive Features in Technology-Enhanced Storybooks: A Meta-Analysis." *Review of Educational Research* 85, no. 4 (2015): 698–739. doi: 10.3102/0034654314566989.

Tamis-LeMonda, Catherine S., Marc H. Bornstein, and Lisa Baumwell. "Maternal Responsiveness and Children's Achievement of Language Milestones." *Child Development* 72, no. 3 (2001): 748–67. doi: 10.1111/1467-8624.00313.

Tamis-LeMonda, Catherine S., Yana Kuchirko, and Lulu Song. "Why Is Infant Language Learning Facilitated by Parental Responsiveness?" *Current Directions in Psychological Science* 23, no. 2 (2014): 121–26. doi: 10.1177/0963721414522813.

Teague, Mark. *Jack and the Beanstalk and the French Fries*. New York: Scholastic, 2018.

Tomasello, Michael. *Constructing A Language: A Usage-Based Theory of Language Acquisition*. Cambridge, MA: Harvard University Press, 2003.

Torgesen, Joseph, and Patricia Mathes. *A Basic Guide to Understanding, Assessing, and Teaching Phonological Awareness*. Austin, TX: Pro-Ed, 2000.

Valdez-Menchaca, Marta C., and Grover J. Whitehurst. "Accelerating Language Development Through Picture Book Reading: A Systematic Extension to Mexican Day Care." *Developmental Psychology* 28, no. 6 (1992): 1106–14.

van Kleek, Anne. "Cultural Issues in Promoting Interactive Book Sharing." In *Sharing Books and Stories to Promote Language and Literacy*, edited by Anne van Kleek, 179–230. San Diego, CA: Plural, 2006.

Verhoeven, Ludo, Jan van Leeuwe, and Anne Vermeer. "Vocabulary Growth and Reading Development across the Elementary School Years." *Scientific Studies of Reading* 15, no. 1 (2011): 8–25.

Wasik, Barbara A., and Annemarie H. Hindman. "Realizing the Promise of Open-Ended Questions." *The Reading Teacher* 67, no. 4 (2013): 302–311. doi: 10.1002/trtr.1218.

Wasik, Barbara A., and Annemarie H. Hindman. "Why Wait? The Importance of Wait Time in Developing Young Students' Language and Vocabulary Skills." *Reading Teacher* 72, no. 3 (2018): 369–78. doi: 10.1002/trtr.1730.

Wasik, Barbara A., Annemarie H. Hindman, and Emily K. Snell. "Book Reading and Vocabulary Development: A Systematic Review." *Early Childhood Research Quarterly* 37 (2016): 39–57. doi: 10.1016/j.ecresq.2016.04.003.

Weisleder, Adriana, and Anne Fernald. "Talking to Children Matters: Early Language Experience Strengthens Processing and Builds Vocabulary." *Psychological Science* 24, no. 11 (2013): 2143–52. doi: 10.1177/0956797613488145.

Wexler, Natalie. *The Knowledge Gap*. New York: Avery, 2019.

Whitehurst, Grover J., David S. Arnold, Jeffery N. Epstein, Andrea L. Angell, Meagan Smith, and Janet E. Fischel. "A Picture Book Reading Intervention in Day Care and Home for Children from Low-Income Families." *Developmental Psychology* 30, no. 5 (1994): 679–89.

Whitehurst, Grover J., Deane A. Crone, Andrea A. Zevenbergen, Margaret D. Schultz, Olivia N. Velting, and Janet E. Fischel. "Outcomes of an Emergent Literacy Intervention from Head Start through Second Grade." *Journal of Educational Psychology* 91, no. 2 (1999): 261–72.

Whitehurst, Grover J., Jeffrey N. Epstein, Andrea L. Angell, Adam C. Payne, Deanne A. Crone, and Janet E. Fischel. "Outcomes of an Emergent Literacy Intervention in Head Start." *Journal of Educational Psychology* 86, no. 4 (1994): 542.

Whitehurst, Grover J., Francine L. Falco, Christopher J. Lonigan, Janet E. Fischel, Barbara D. DeBaryshe, Marta C. Valdez-Menchaca, and Marie Caulfield. "Accelerating Language Development through Picture Book Reading." *Developmental Psychology* 24, no. 4 (1988): 552–559.

Willingham, Daniel. *Raising Kids Who Read: What Parents and Teachers Can Do*. San Francisco, CA: Jossey-Bass, 2015.

Wood, David, Jerome S. Bruner, and Gail Ross. "The Role of Tutoring in Problem Solving." *Journal of Child Psychology & Psychiatry* 17 (1976): 89–100.

Yamada, Kobi. *What Do You Do With an Idea?* Seattle, WA: Compendium, 2014.

———. *What Do You Do With a Problem?* Seattle, WA: Compendium, 2016.

Zentall, Shannon R., and Bradley J. Morris. "'Good Job, You're so Smart': The Effects of Inconsistency of Praise Type on Young Children's Motivation." *Journal of Experimental Child Psychology* 107, no. 2 (2010): 155–63. doi: 10.1016/j.jecp.2010.04.015.

Zevenbergen, Andrea, and Grover Whitehurst. "Dialogic Reading: A Shared Picture Book Intervention for Preschoolers." In *On Reading Books to Children: Parents and Teachers*, edited by Anne van Kleek, Steven Stahl and Eurydice Bauer, 177–200. Mahwah, NJ: Lawrence Erlbaum Associates, 2003.

Ziegler, Johannes C, and Usha Goswami. "Reading Acquisition, Developmental Dyslexia, and Skilled Reading across Languages: A Psycholinguistic Grain Size Theory." *Psychological Bulletin* 131, no. 1 (2005): 3–29. doi: 10.1037/0033-2909.131.1.3.

Index

Page references for figures are italicized.

alphabetic principle, 3–5
alphabet knowledge, 2, 84
Anderson, Richard C., 9

Beck, Isabel, 17, 44
book handling skills, 2, 84

concepts about print, 3, 42, 84
contextualized language, 43

decodable books, 54
decode, 5, 6, 42, 73, 74
decoding, 1, 5–8, 14, 74
decontextualized language, 43, 46
dialogic reading, original approach, 13, 14, 15, 19, 20, 31, 33, 36, 53, 72, 74
distancing. *See* EMPOWERED strategies, distancing
distractions, 72

electronic books, 59–60
EMPOWERED strategies:
 distancing, *17*, 18, 19, *26–29*, 32, 36–37, 46, 54, 66, 67, 70, 72, 73, 76, 79, *81–84*;
 encourage vocabulary, *16*, 17, 18, *26–29*, 29–30, 66, 67, 73, *81–83*; evaluation, *17*, 19, *26–29*, 35–36, 67, 68, *81–84*; expansion, *16*, 19, *26–29*, 32–34, 37, 46, 66–67, *81–84*; make it fun, *16*, 29–30, 46, 60–61, 67, 68, 74, 76; open-ended questions, *16*, 18, *26–29*, 32–33, 46, 49, 60, 66–70, 73, 79, *81–84*; prompt frequently, *16*, 18, 30–31, 67, 79, *81–84*; repetition, *17*, 19, *26–29*, 34–35, 37, 46, 66–68, 76, *81–84*; wh-questions, *16*, 18, *26–29*, 32–33, 37, 46, 48, 49, 57, 60, 66–70, 73, 76, 79, *81–84*
encourage vocabulary. *See* EMPOWERED strategies, encourage vocabulary
evaluation. *See* EMPOWERED strategies, evaluation
expansions, 41

expansion. *See* EMPOWERED strategies, expansion

fluency, 6

Gough, Philip, 1

independent reading level, 54
Irwin, Julia, 82
language comprehension, 1, 14, 20–21
Lonigan, Christopher J., 87

make it fun. *See* EMPOWERED strategies, make it fun
Matthew effect, 9
Moats, Lousia, 85

Nagy, William, 9
nonfiction books, 58–59

open-ended questions. *See* EMPOWERED strategies, open-ended questions
orthographic mapping, 5, 87

phonemic awareness, 4
phonics instruction, 5–6, 10; systematic phonics, 6
phonological awareness, 3–5, 61, 84
phonological sensitivity, 4
prompt frequently. *See* EMPOWERED strategies, prompt frequently

reading comprehension, 1, 6–9, 15, 20, 42, 85
repetition. *See* EMPOWERED strategies, repetition

scaffolding, 18, 35, 36, 46, 70–71, 76
science of reading, 2, 85–86
Seidenberg, Mark, 84, 86
Shanahan, Timothy, 86
simple view of reading, 1
Stanovich, Keith, 9
Stone, Lyn, 87

three-cueing, 86
tier 2 words, 17, 44, 47, 59
Tunmer, William, 1

use of pictures, 49–50, 55, 72–74

vocabulary, 6–8, 10, 15, 18; breadth versus depth, 7, 41; encourage vocabulary. *See* EMPOWERED strategies, encourage vocabulary; expressive vocabulary, 6, 7, 9, 42; receptive vocabulary, 6, 7, 42; vocabulary instruction, 7
vocabulary spurt, 42

wait time, 71, 76
Wexler, Natalie, 84
Whitehurst, Grover J., 13, 14, 19, 87
wh-questions. *See* EMPOWERED strategies, wh-questions
Willingham, Daniel, 85
word recognition, 5, 14, 74

About the Authors

Dr. Dina Moore is associate professor of psychology and codirector of the Reading Evaluation And Development of Skills (READS) laboratory at Southern Connecticut State University. Her research interests are reading skill in college-aged students and literacy development and intervention in young readers. She is also the coauthor of the book *Preparing Children for Reading Success: Hands-On Activities for Librarians, Educators, and Caregivers*.

Dr. Cheryl C. Durwin is professor of psychology and codirector of the Reading Evaluation And Development of Skills (READS) laboratory at Southern Connecticut State University. As an educational psychologist, her research focus is on reading acquisition and the development and validation of reading assessments and interventions. She is also the coauthor of the textbook *EdPsych Modules*, 4th edition.